PENNSYLVANIA GLASSWARE, *1870–1904*

Distributed by Charles Scribner's Sons, New York

Pennsylvania Glassware
1870–1904

Pressed tumblers, stem ware, patterned sets, cruets,
jars; etched and cut glass globes, shades, stalactites, balls;
flint glass flasks, brandies, whiskeys, decanters, bitters,
condiment bottles, jars; cut glass bowls, celeries, carafes, decanters,
jugs, tankards, nappies, bon-bons, goblets, tumblers

KING, SON & COMPANY, EARLY 1870's
(CASCADE GLASSWORKS)
PHOENIX GLASS COMPANY, 1893
THE AGNEW COMPANY, LTD., 1894
T. B. CLARK & COMPANY, 1896
UNITED STATES GLASS COMPANY, 1904

Compiled by the Editors of The Pyne Press

AMERICAN HISTORICAL CATALOG COLLECTION

THE PYNE PRESS
Princeton

Pennsylvania Glassware
1870–1904

an historical introduction

No area of the United States is more closely identified with glassmaking than the State of Pennsylvania, in particular, that section known to the industry as the Pittsburgh district. Blown, pressed, cut, etched—every variety of process, every nuance of form, nearly every style of decoration known to glassmakers and collectors was employed at one time in the manufacture of Pennsylvania glass. The efforts of New Jersey, Massachusetts, New York, Ohio and West Virginia glasshouses have been no less notable, but neither have they been so concentrated and comprehensive.

What accounts for this concentration of glassmaking activity? The reasons are primarily economic. The earliest Pennsylvania glasshouses were founded, most naturally, in the Philadelphia area. These were related in time and situation to the South Jersey glassworks across the Delaware. The first mention of a Pennsylvania glasshouse occurs in Philadelphia records from 1683, but nothing is known about this early enterprise. The first important Pennsylvania glasshouse was established by Henry William Stiegel, a German émigré from Cologne, in Manheim in 1763. It was a large enterprise employing 130 workmen, many of them fellow German glassmen with a thorough knowledge of continental manufacturing methods. They produced what has been called "American Flint Glass," although the product did not always contain lead. Tableware, bottles and window glass—much of it of extremely fine quality—came from this firm until its closing in 1774. A second important eastern Pennsylvania glasshouse was the Schuylkill Glass Works in the Philadelphia area. Founded in 1780, it flourished in the 1790's under the superintendency of William Peter Eichbaum, a German emigrant. His move in 1797 to Pittsburgh with another glassmaker, Frederick Wendt, to direct a new enterprise, the Pittsburgh Glass Works, founded by James O'Hara and Issac Craig, marks the beginning of the rapid rise of the Pittsburgh-area glass industry.

Today, glass can be made literally anywhere. In the late eighteenth and early nineteenth centuries, readily available sources of fuel (first wood, and, increasingly, after 1807, coal), such raw ingredients as sand and alkalis, skilled labor, and convenient, inexpensive means of transportation were critical. The Pittsburgh area was ideal in almost every respect. The skilled German, Irish and English glassmakers were attracted to this new region. William Price, an English glassblower, was hired in 1800 by O'Hara to make flint glass. He failed at first but success was not far off. In 1805 John Frederick Amelung, who had established the "New Bremen Glass Manufactory" at Frederick, Maryland, in 1784, joined the Pittsburgh Glass Works, now run solely by General O'Hara. Amelung's first venture, which lasted 11 years, was an important source of skilled labor. Many of his laborers decided to join a new glassmaking company started by Albert Gallatin and associates, the New Geneva Glass Works, in a small town outside Pittsburgh, in 1798. Others joined the O'Hara firm and, later, yet newer glasshouses.

Thus, by the very early years of the nineteenth century, two of the most important individuals in the development of the American glass industry and many of their followers had joined the move to the West. With them went a knowledge of glassmaking methods which was unrivaled in America and which was to be refined again and again to take advantage of new sources of fuel, raw materials and a rapidly increasing domestic demand for glass products. Of special interest to the collector today, of course, is the westward movement of patterns, of decorative techniques, of forms which were the inheritance of Old World tradition and learning but which were to become—in mixture—a distinctive American glass imprint.

An advertisement appearing in the *Pittsburgh Gazette* in 1804 is often quoted in books on American glass, and with good reason. It states quite clearly (allowing for some commercial hyperbole) the state of the glassmaking art in the Pittsburgh area at that time:

> The Proprietors of the Pittsburgh Glass Works, having procured a sufficient number of the most approved European Glass manufacturers, and having on hand a large stock of the best materials, on which their workmen are now employed, have the pleasure of assuring the public, that window-glass of a superior quality and of any size from 7x9, to 8x24 inches, carefully packed in boxes containing 100 feet each, may be had at the shortest notice. Glass of large sizes, for other purposes may also be had, such as for pictures, coach glasses, clock faces, &c. Bottles of all kinds of any quantity may also be had, together with pocket flasks, pickling jars, apothecary's shop furniture or other hollow ware, the whole at least 25 per cent lower than articles of the same quality brought from any sea port in the United States. A liberal allowance will be made on sale of large quantities. Orders from merchants and others will be punctually attended to on application to

> or the Store of Prather & Smiley
> Market Street, Pittsburgh

> JAMES O'HARA
> or
> ISSAC CRAIG

Cut pieces from high quality flint glass were produced in the Pittsburgh area very early; Eichbaum was a skilled cutter. But pressed glass articles were to be the primary emphasis, aside from window glass. Among the first firms to specialize in pressed tableware was that founded by Benjamin Bakewell and Edward Ensell in Pittsburgh in 1807. It was first known as Bakewell & Ensell, then as Bakewell & Company; Bakewell & Page; Bakewell, Page & Bakewell; and, finally, by the time of its demise in 1882, as Bakewell, Pears and

Company. The argument as to where, when and by whom pressed glass was first produced is almost as old as the Bakewell firm itself. A patent was issued to John O. Bakewell in 1825 for producing glass furniture knobs. At about the same time, Hiram Dillaway of the Boston and Sandwich Glass Company of East Cambridge, Massachusetts, patented several molds and methods of pressing glassware. It is virtually incontestable, however, in the words of glass expert Albert Christian Revi, that "a much earlier start in pressing glass articles was made in the Pittsburgh area." Part of the problem, as Ruth Webb Lee notes in her classic volume, *Victorian Glass*, is "The persistence of 'Sandwich' as a convenient generic description for all kinds of patterned glass [this] is not to be wondered at so long as tourists will buy any so-called Sandwich glass in Sandwich, and, while they remain within the sacred precincts of Cape Cod, will decline anything offered as Pittsburgh."

In 1818, an English visitor published his observations of an American trip, in *A Narrative of a Journey*, and expressed his surprise, "to witness such perfection on this side of the Atlantic, and especially in that part of America which a New Yorker supposes to be at the farther end of the world. At Messrs. Page & Bakewell's glass warehouse I saw chandeliers and numerous articles in cut glass of a very splendid description; . . . It is well to bear in mind that the demand for these articles of elegant beauty lies in the western states! the inhabitants of Eastern America being still importers from the Old Country."

These imports would begin to decline in the 1840's, especially with the introduction of complete settings in pressed ware by pattern. Pressed ware has been America's great contribution to glass technology and it virtually revolutionized the market for glass products. From the 1830's on, new techniques were developed to speed if not improve the production of pressed glass by the introduction of new molds, raw materials, presses and furnaces. Prior to the Civil War, almost all the ware was made of flint glass, the use of lime glass, a cheaper substitute, having not yet been introduced. No one can claim that the pressed glassware of Bakewell or such other firms in Pittsburgh of the 1850's as Bryce, McKee and Company or Atterbury & Company can compare with the blown wares of Stiegel, but their beauty and utility were to be valued for many years, and have been revalued in recent years. As Marvin Schwartz writes in his survey of American glass (*Collector's Guide to Antique American Glass*), "Curiously enough in the field of glass the distinctive American product remained important and skillful, if occasionally a little revolting to serious estheticians."

Most glassmaking firms, unlike Bakewell, managed to survive, at most, a dozen years. Not until the end of the Civil War was the industry to stabilize itself to any great degree. By that time, gas was being used as the principal fuel, rather than coal, and this was a less expensive and more efficient medium. The glass manufacturers of western Pennsylvania were, of course, in a unique position to take advantage of this technological development. In the late 1850's and throughout the '60's, a number of Pittsburgh-based firms came into existence, many of them utilizing the economic know-how and production expertise developed at the Bakewell enterprise. Among these new companies were Atterbury & Company; Campbell, Jones & Company; Challinor, Taylor & Company; The Crystal Glass Company; Doyle & Company; Richards & Hartley; Ripley & Co.; and the Cascade Glass Company. Cascade was founded in 1859. In 1864 it was reorganized as Johnson, King and Company, and in 1869, it was known as King, Son & Company.

KING, SON & COMPANY
Cascade Glass Works

King was a manufacturer of pressed, blown and cut glassware. It was for its pressed ware, however, that the company was best known. As noted earlier, patterned sets of pressed tableware were introduced by 1840, and such sets were produced in the thousands by many glasshouses in the period following the Civil War. Lime glass replaced flint at this time, although cut glass was still being produced from flint; often, as the years passed, with the use of blanks.

Most experts on pressed ware speak of three or four design periods or styles, the first being Empire or neo-classical, popular until the 1830's. The second, Rococo, was fashionable until the Civil War; and the third, Gothic, enjoyed a vogue until the turn of the century. One might say that there was a fourth period at the beginning of the 1900's, the Eclectic or Fussy. By 1900, the trend had become over-elaborate, and more simple patterns employing "Colonial" or neo-classic forms started reappearing. As Marvin Schwartz has stated, "Pressed glass is the medium in which problems in taste are blatantly manifested; it was created a luxury available to all, and was often designed to attract the casual buyer rather than the serious esthetician."

The sets shown in the King, Son & Company pages are clearly from the early years of the 1870's and reflect "Gothic" Victorian tastes. A "Gothic" pattern first appeared about 1860, and all major pressed glass manufacturers offered some variant thereof. King called their set "Gothic Ware" (p. 27). Their most famous pattern was the "Maple," a design of which was patented by William C. King in 1871 (p. 22). It has been mistakenly called "Hops Band" and is a variant of the "Paneled Grape Band" pattern. King provided a description of his design in the patent papers: "Long inclosed panels or spaces containing a succession of raised Maple leaves overlapping each other and pointing in opposite directions, or towards the ends of panels, the last two leaves being base to base at the center of the panel and having their stems crossed." The squares between the panels were "occupied by rosettes," and the finials for covered pieces were pine cones.

Many of the designs featured in the catalog pages were first produced in the early years of the 70's. One of the most interesting of these is the "Floral Ware," "New and Old Set" (also known as "Bleeding Heart," Ruth Webb Lee, *Early American Pressed Glass*, pattern 154). According to Miss Lee, the Sandwich company also made a "Bleeding Heart" pattern. This is illustrated on page 26 of the catalog. The "Centennial" pattern (p. 34) was probably introduced earlier than the centennial year. The plate is clearly marked "Patented," and King and August Sperber did patent a mold for curved and ribbed "shell feet," the type which appear on the "Centennial" pieces, in 1875.

In general, the patterns illustrated in the King catalog are simple, only slightly "Gothic" in feeling. On page 38 the reader will find some of the patterns of engraving which could be applied; they are relatively subdued. This applies, too, to the many goblets which King supplied (illustrated on p. 22). Among these are the "Huber" pattern (Lee, *Early American Pressed Glass*, pattern 15), "Lattice" (Lee, *Early American Pressed Glass*, pattern 247), "Argus" (Lee, *Early American Pressed Glass*, pattern 2), the "Maple," "Floral" and "Gothic." There is no doubt that the King company owed much of its originality to such earlier manufacturers as Bakewell, especially for the "Argus" and "Huber" patterns. King, Son & Co. was a fine pressed glassware manufacturer, but not a terribly original one. Much of their work had been done for them.

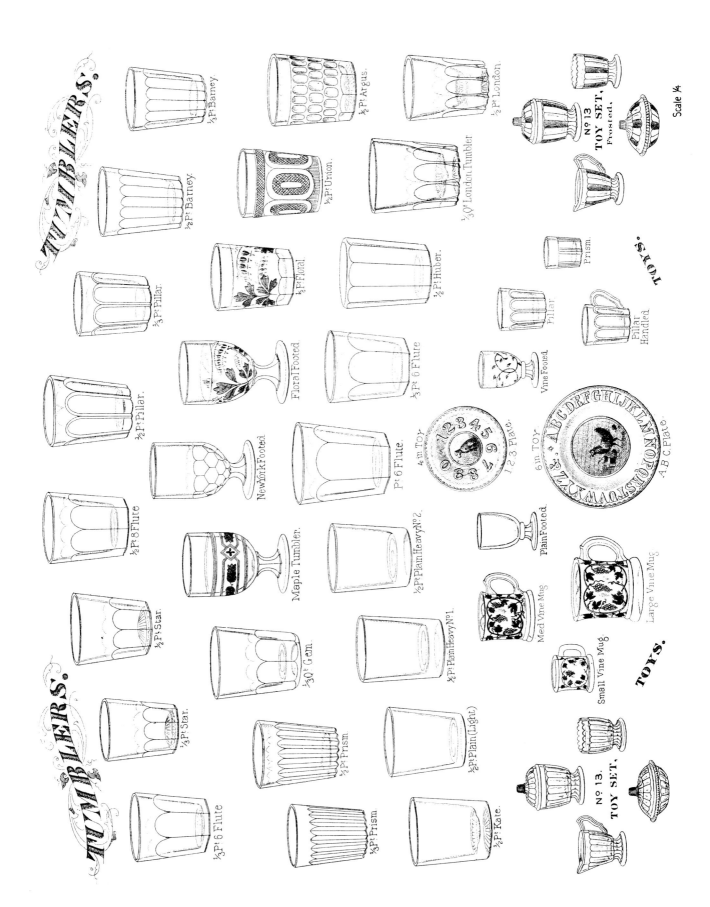

TUMBLERS.

⅓ Pt Barney.
½ Pt Barney.
⅓ Pt Pillar.
½ Pt Pillar.
½ Pt Pillar.
½ Pt 8 Flute.
½ Pt Star.
⅓ Pt Star.

½ Pt Argus.
½ Pt Union.
½ Pt Floral.
Floral Footed.
New York Footed.
Maple Tumbler.
⅓ Qt Gem.
½ Pt Prism.
⅓ Pt Prism.

½ Pt London.
⅓ Qt London Tumbler.
½ Pt Huber.
½ Pt 6 Flute.
Pt 6 Flute.
½ Pt Plain Heavy No 2.
½ Pt Plain Heavy No 1.
½ Pt Plain (Light).

TUMBLERS.

½ Pt 6 Flute.
½ Pt Kate.

Nº 13
TOY SET,
Frosted.

TOYS.

Prism.
Pillar.
Pillar Handled.
Vine Footed.
Plain Footed.

4 in Toy.
1.2.3 Plate.
6 in Toy.
A.B.C. Plate.

ABCDEFGHIJKLMN OPQRSTUVWXYZ &.

Med Vine Mug.
Large Vine Mug.
Small Vine Mug.

TOYS.

Nº 13.
TOY SET,

Scale ¼

T. B. CLARK & COMPANY

It is a curious commentary on the vagaries of fashion that the once despised pressed glass is in demand today, while the expensive cut glass so popular for wedding gifts a generation ago, is not wanted by experienced collectors today.
— Ruth Webb Lee, in EARLY AMERICAN
PRESSED GLASS

Curious, indeed, for now cut glass is in great demand, and is being reproduced by every cutter who managed to survive the slump of the 1920's through the 50's. While not yet the staple item for a new bride that it was in the late Victorian era, it is valued by young collectors, many of whom have scoured their grandparents' attic for neglected pieces.

Cut glass experts have defined four different periods of design: (1) the Rococo and neo-classical (1770–1820), (2) Empire (1820–40), (3) Rococo and Renaissance revivals (1840–1880), and (4) the Brilliant period. Stiegel produced the first Pennsylvania cut glass items, and John Frederick Amelung, a cutter, brought the art to the Pittsburgh area. Bakewell was the leading Pittsburgh producer in the mid-nineteenth century, and Gillinder and Sons of Philadelphia excelled in the eastern part of the state. The Philadelphia Centennial of 1876 helped to create a vogue for the cut wares; Gillinder set up a complete glassworks on the exhibition grounds. By this time, most of the glass furnaces, at least in the Pittsburgh area, had been converted to gas, a fuel which produced a much clearer, brighter flint glass highly suitable for cutting. As the glass became purer and purer, the designs cut into them became more complex and intriguing. New equipment for brushing and cutting was also introduced and by the 1890's much of this was electrified.

Although the Gillinder firm itself moved to the Pittsburgh area in 1883, the cut glass industry, increasingly specialized, was not so highly concentrated geographically as that of the pressed. Many more manufacturers were located in New York State, including such justly famous firms as L. Straus & Sons (New York City), J. Hoare & Co. (Corning), and T. G. Hawkes, later Steuben Glass Works (Corning). Increasingly, cut glass manufacturers worked from flint glass blanks supplied by other companies. This was the case with T. B. Clark & Co.

Thomas Byron Clark came to Honesdale, Pennsylvania, in 1884 to start a cut glass business close to that founded by Christian Dorflinger nineteen years earlier at White Mills, Wayne County. By the 1890's, Dorflinger was employing several hundred workers, and Honesdale, in northeastern Pennsylvania, had become famous as an important American cut glass center. According to Albert Christian Revi, "The Dorflinger glassworks supplied crystal and cased colored blanks for cutting and engraving to more than 22 cutting shops in their area."

Clark became second only to Dorflinger as a producer in the region. During the late 1880's and throughout the 90's they could supply any housewife with the standard pieces in a cut table setting, a setting which might include goblets, wines (champagne, claret and sherry), ice cream dishes and plates with ice cream platter, finger bowls with plates, salts and peppers, candlesticks, butter patties, compotes, bonbon or nut dishes, celery boats, several nappies of various sizes, berry bowls, punch cups and pickle dishes.

Several important designs originated at the Clark factory, including the "Strawberry-Diamond and Star," created by Walter A. Wood, Clark's brother-in-law; "Baker's

T. B. CLARK & COMPANY'S AMERICAN CUT GLASS.

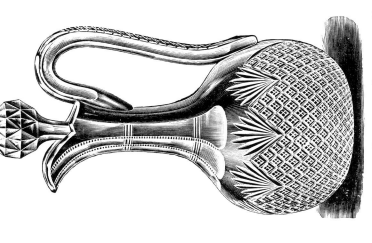

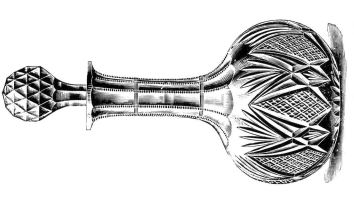

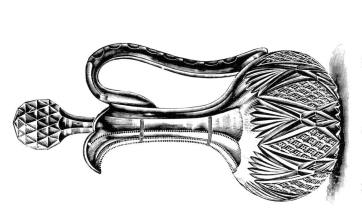

Quart Handled Decanter, Winola.
$12.00.

Quart No Handle Decanter, Winola.
$10.00.

Quart Handled Decanter, Straw and Fan.
$14.00.   Without Handle $12.00.

Gothic," designed by Thomas A. Baker and the first of the "Gothic" cut glass designs (1888); "Six Sea Shells," a Wood design (1892). All the articles in the catalog are marked as to price. As is readily apparent, they were not inexpensive, nor should they have been. They were the work of real craftsmen. It is estimated that a 9-inch berry bowl, not unlike those illustrated on page 109, which cost $35 in 1900 would cost $100 to reproduce today.

Variations on the "Strawberry-Diamond with Fan" pattern were staples of the Brilliant cut glass period and of the Clark line. Individual pieces are not, however, identified according to general pattern name but by commercial name, except for the quart-size handled decanter (p. 114), "Straw and Fan." The most popular of the Clark commercial lines would seem to have been the "Winola," "Manhattan," "Jewel" and "Desdemona." In each, the popular deep cut diamond pattern emerges.

A few pieces employ silver fittings (see p. 123) which were probably made by Clark at his Wayne Silver Company in Honesdale, established in 1895.

PHOENIX GLASS COMPANY

Some flint glassware producers stayed alive following the introduction of lime glass by turning to the production of shades and lamps. Not until after the Philadelphia Centennial was there much of a demand for fine cut glass. Phoenix, founded in 1880, began producing good cut glass immediately, and in the 1890's expanded into the field of gas and electric globes, shades, balls, bowls, etc. And they became one of the leaders of the field.

Some of the pieces illustrated in the catalog pages are cut, but a great majority of them are etched. Phoenix was fortunate in acquiring the services of a master English etcher, Joseph Webb. Familiar cut glass patterns are represented; the etched designs are very rich and colorful. The plain globes are rare, and only a few employ literal designs such as those of Masonic or GAR motif (p. 47).

Until a few years ago, objects such as these usually ended up on the scrap heap. Their use today in the manner for which they were intended is rare. Collectors, however, have found new and imaginative decorative uses.

THE AGNEW COMPANY, LTD.

Flint glass bottles such as those produced by Agnew and hundreds of other small glasshouses in the 1890's were a dime a dozen. Now they are the object of much search. They are among the most utilitarian of American glass products and possess a very modern, clean appeal. Those produced by Agnew were in no way extraordinary but neither were those of larger commercial glassware manufacturers whose products are eagerly sought today.

The Agnew catalog pages provide the reader with a basic primer of late-19th century bottle designs. It has been said, "As time went on, bottles generally were made thinner and thinner." This would appear to be true if one compares these pages with those from earlier commercial glass catalogs. The bottles are, of course, shown without lettered plates. It is amusing to note that the manufacturer instructed his customers (p. 73) that "Long inscriptions detract from the appearance of the bottles, and are not recommended."

Pittsburgh Oval.   Washington Oval.

PITTSBURGH OVALS.

8 oz.	1 Gross Boxes,			Per gross,	$14 00
16 oz.	½	...	-	-	.... 23 00
30 oz.	½	...	-	-	.... 36 00
32 oz.	½	....	-	-	.... 36 00

WASHINGTON OVALS.

8 oz.	1 Gross Boxes,			Per gross,	$14 00
16 oz.	½	....	-	-	.... 23 00
32 oz.	½	....	-	-	.... 36 00

UNITED STATES GLASS COMPANY

The United States Glass Company, the result of a merger of 18 Western Pennsylvania, Eastern Ohio and West Virginia glass companies (listed on p. 133), rode the vogue for pressed tableware sets to death. The giant began with some of the finest of the Wheeling and Pittsburgh firms, and by 1904 only six of them were left as producers. Significantly, five of the six were and, had been before the merger, Pittsburgh-based factory operations. Since 1891 U. S. Glass had added three new factories, Factory D, a gold-decorating plant; Factory H, a plate-etching plant; and Factory U, a tank operation at Gas City, Indiana.

The giant corporation continued to offer some of the old patterns and the reader will find one pattern, "Pennsylvania" (also known as the "Hand Pattern"), made by the O'Hara Glass Company, and a second, "Oregon," made by Richards and Hartley. Two other patterns — "Wisconsin," (also known as "Beaded Dewdrop") and "Indiana" — are known to have been produced at the Gas City plant (Factory U).

U. S. Glass made almost anything available in the substance — birdbaths, globes and shades, ink bottles, lamps, paper weights, but tableware was its staple. Most of the patterned sets carried state names, a practice which seems to have begun in the 1890's. At this time the company produced a series of six "battleship" patterns: "Ohio," "Maryland," "Kentucky" (not included in this catalog) and "Pennsylvania," "Michigan" and "Illinois" (included). Many of the patterned sets can be dated with some accuracy.

The "California" (also known as the "Beaded Grape") was introduced c. 1895, and was available in emerald green and clear. The "Colonial" (also known as "United States") was first available c. 1891. "Colorado" was probably introduced in 1897. "Columbia" is dated by some as c. 1907, but it was clearly available earlier. "Georgia" (also known as "Peacock Feather") may have been offered as early as 1895. "Kansas" (known also as "Jewel and Dewdrop") was originally produced by the Co-Operative Flint Glass Company of Beaver Falls, and was probably introduced in the U. S. Glass line in the late 90's. "Manhattan" dates from c. 1902; "Missouri," c. 1891; "Texas," c. 1900; "Virginia," c. 1895 (after 1906 known as the "Mirror" pattern); "Wyoming," c. 1900; and "Victor" (known today as "Shell and Jewel") was produced originally by the Westmoreland Glass Co. of Grapeville in 1893.

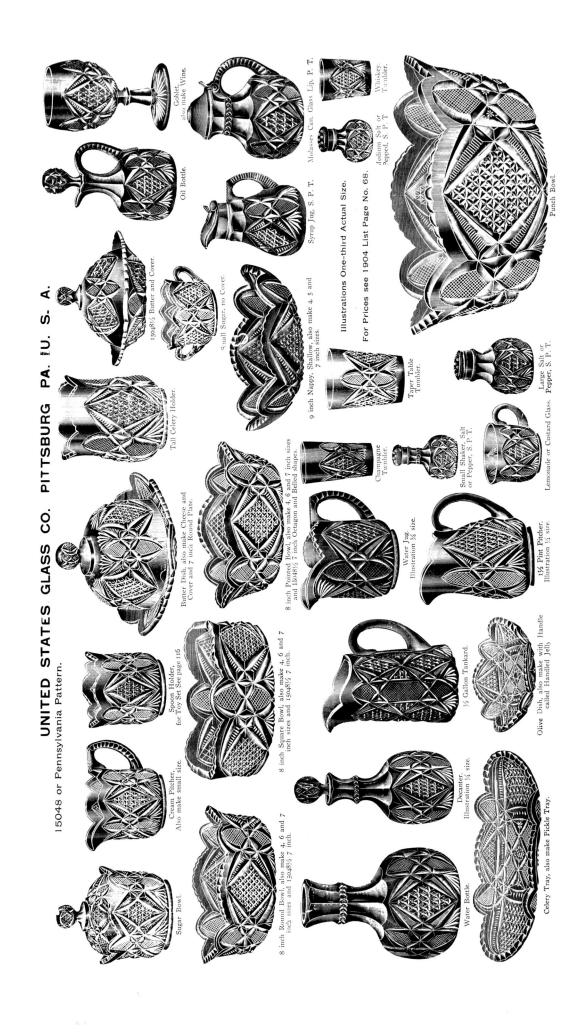

UNITED STATES GLASS CO. PITTSBURG PA. U. S. A.

15048 or Pennsylvania Pattern.

Goblet, also make Wine.

Oil Bottle.

Whiskey Tumbler.

Molasses Can. Glass Lip, P. T.

Medium Salt or Pepper, S. P. T.

Syrup Jug, S. P. T.

Illustrations One-third Actual Size.

For Prices see 1904 List Page No. 68.

Punch Bowl.

1504 8½ Butter and Cover.

Small Sugar, no Cover.

9 inch Nappy, Shallow, also make 4, 5 and 7 inch sizes.

Taper Table Tumbler.

Large Salt or Pepper, S. P. T.

Tall Celery Holder.

Butter Dish, also make Cheese and Cover and 7 inch Round Plate.

8 inch Pointed Bowl, also make 4, 6 and 7 inch sizes and 15048½ 7 inch Octagon and Belled shapes.

Champagne Tumbler.

Small Shaker, Salt or Pepper, S. P. T.

Lemonade or Custard Glass.

Spoon Holder, for Toy Set See page 116.

8 inch Square Bowl, also make 4, 6 and 7 inch sizes and 15048½ 7 inch.

Water Jug. Illustration ½ size.

1½ Pint Pitcher. Illustration ¼ size.

Cream Pitcher, Also make small size.

½ Gallon Tankard.

Olive Dish, also make with Handle called Handled Jelly.

Sugar Bowl.

8 inch Round Bowl, also make 4, 6 and 7 inch sizes and 15048½ 7 inch.

Decanter, Illustration ¼ size.

Water Bottle.

Celery Tray, also make Pickle Tray.

Suggestions for further reading

DANIEL, DOROTHY. *Cut and Engraved Glass, 1771–1905.* New York: M. Barrows and Co., 1950.

DAVIS, PEARCE. *The Development of the American Glass Industry.* Cambridge, Mass.: Harvard University Press, 1949.

FREEMAN, DR. LARRY. *Grand Old American Bottles.* Watkins Glen, N.Y.: Century House, 1964.

KENDRICK, GRACE. *The Antique Bottle Collector.* Sparks, Nev.: Western Printing and Publishing, 1964.

KNITTLE, RHEA MANSFIELD. *Early American Glass.* New York: Appleton-Century, 1934.

LEE, RUTH WEBB. *Early American Pressed Glass.* Enlarged and revised edition. Wellesley, Mass.: Lee Publications, 1931.

LEE, RUTH WEBB. *Victorian Glass.* Wellesley, Mass.: Lee Publications, 1944.

McKEARIN, GEORGE S. and HELEN. *American Glass.* New York: Crown, 1948.

REVI, ALBERT CHRISTIAN. *American Cut and Engraved Glass.* Camden, N.J.: Thomas Nelson, 1965.

REVI, ALBERT CHRISTIAN. *American Pressed Glass and Figure Bottles.* Camden, N.J.: Thomas Nelson, 1964.

SCHWARTZ, MARVIN. *Collector's Guide to Antique American Glass.* New York: Doubleday, 1969.

Important public collections

Many museums, historical societies and historic homes open to the public hold and display examples of mid- to late-nineteenth century Pennsylvania glass of all varieties. Most of the major collections listed below stress examples dated prior to 1860, but may include unusual items of later date.

Brooklyn Museum, Brooklyn, New York
Carnegie Institute, Museum of Art, Pittsburgh, Penn.
Chrysler Museum, Institute of Glass, Provincetown, Mass.
Cincinnati Art Museum, Cincinnati, Ohio
Corning Museum of Glass, Corning, New York
Henry Ford Museum, Greenfield Village, Dearborn, Mich.
Henry Francis du Pont Winterthur Museum, Winterthur, Del.
Metropolitan Museum, New York, New York
Philadelphia Museum of Art, Philadelphia, Penn.
Toledo Museum of Art, Toledo, Ohio
Wadsworth Atheneum, Hartford, Conn.

THE CATALOGS

KING, SON & COMPANY
(Cascade Glass Works)

The crystal glassware catalog of King, Son & Co. is undated but surely was produced between 1870 and 1875, and is representative of the firm's middle period. William C. King bought the five-year-old Cascade Glass Company of Pittsburgh in 1864, and the firm was renamed Johnson, King & Co. The Cascade Glass Works identity, however, was maintained for many years. In 1869 the name was changed to King, Son & Co., and in 1880 to King Glass Co.

The firm was one of the major Pittsburgh manufacturers of pressed, blown and cut glass. King, himself, patented one important design for pressed ware ("Maple") and registered three patents for special pressed ware molds. This glasshouse was one of the 18 which merged in 1891 to form the United States Glass Company. It was also among the few member companies to survive the great strike of 1893–96, and was identified in early 1900's U. S. Glass literature as "Factory K."

Among the pressed patterns of special interest to collectors on the following pages are "Union" ("Banded Buckle"), "Maple" and "Floral Ware" ("Bleeding Heart"). The only illustration from the original not included is one showing offerings of the company's very minor lines (plate No. 25): tinctures, salt mouths, graduates, and fluted and plain lamps.

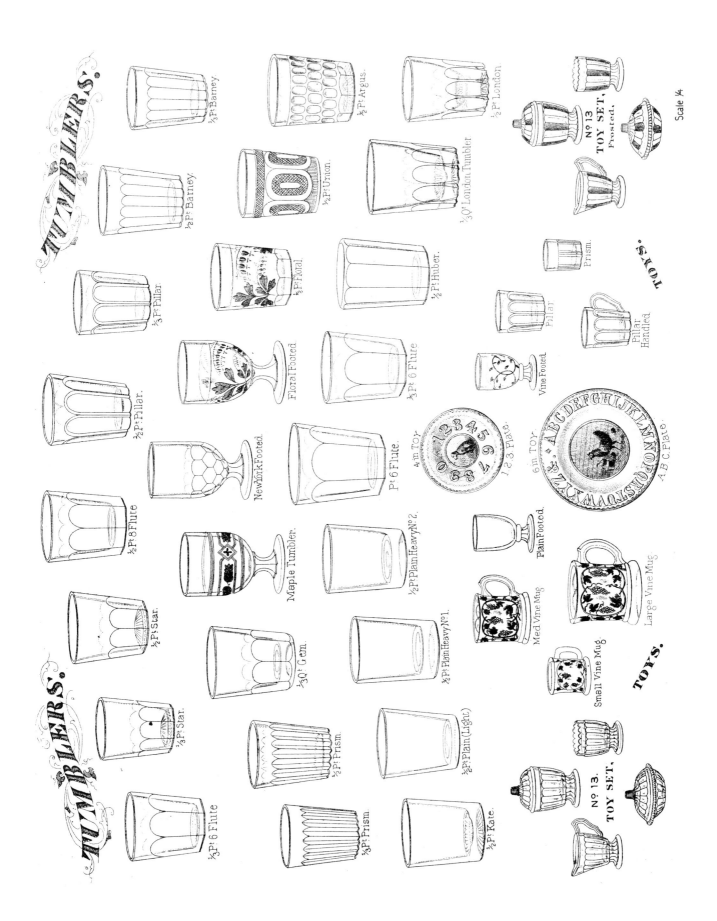

TUMBLERS.

⅓ Pt Barney.

½ Pt Argus.

½ Pt London

⅓ Pt Barney.

½ Pt Union.

½Qt London Tumbler

⅓ Pt Pillar.

⅓ Pt Floral

½ Pt Huber.

½ Pt Pillar.

Floral Footed

½ Pt 6 Flute

½ Pt 8 Flute

New York Footed.

Pt 6 Flute.

½ Pt Star.

Maple Tumbler.

½ Pt Plain Heavy Nº 2.

⅓ Pt Star.

½ Qt Gem.

½ Pt Plain Heavy Nº 1.

TUMBLERS.

⅓ Pt Star.

½ Pt Prism.

½ Pt Plain (Light)

⅓ Pt 6 Flute

⅓ Pt Prism.

½ Pt Kate.

TOYS.

Nº 13
TOY SET.
Frosted.

Scale ¼

Prism.

Pillar

Pillar
Handled

Vine Footed

4 in. Toy.
1 2 3 4 5 6 7 8 9 0

1. 2. 3. Plate.

6 in. Toy.
ABCDEFGHIJKLMNOPQRSTUVWXYZ&.

A B C. Plate.

Plain Footed.

Large Vine Mug.

Med Vine Mug

Small Vine Mug.

TOYS.

Nº 13.
TOY SET.

18

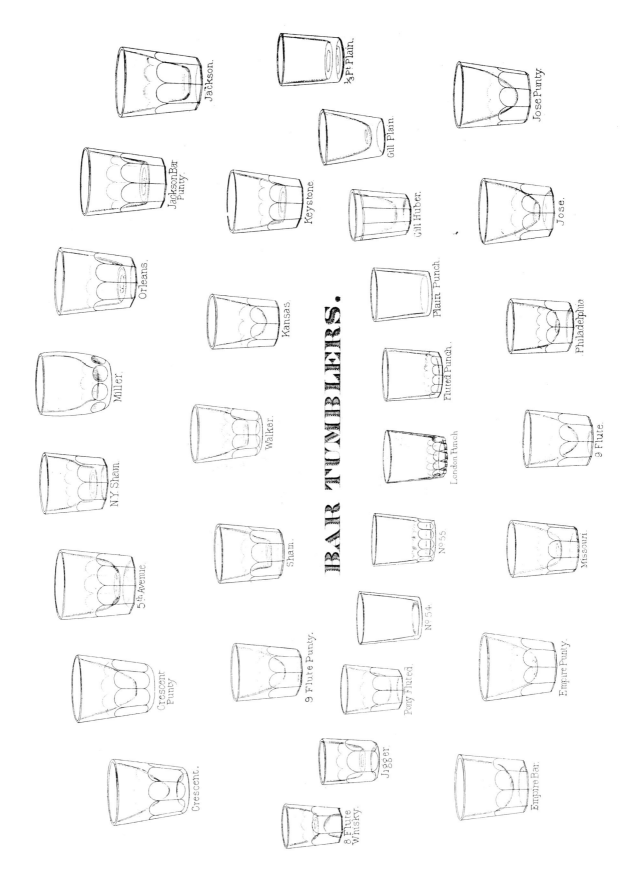

BAR TUMBLERS.

Jackson.

⅔ Pt Plain.

Jose Punty

Scale ¼

JacksonBar Punty.

Keystone.

Gill Plain.

Gill Huber.

Jose.

Orleans.

Kansas

Plain Punch.

Philadelphia

Miller.

Fluted Punch.

N.Y. Sham.

Walker.

London Punch

9 Flute.

5th Avenue

Sham.

Nº 55

Missouri.

Crescent Punty

9 Flute Punty.

Nº 54

Empire Punty.

Pony Fluted

Crescent.

Jigger

Empire Bar.

8 Flute Whisky.

19

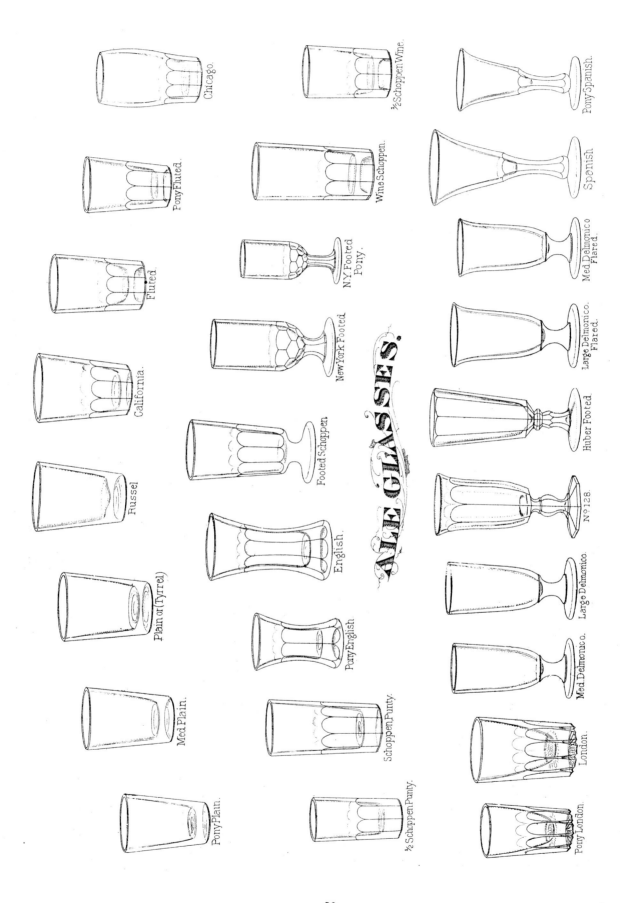

Chicago.

Pony Fluted.

Fluted.

California.

Russel

Plain or (Tyrrel)

Med. Plain.

Pony Plain.

½ Schoppen Wine.

Wine Schoppen.

N.Y. Footed Pony.

New York Footed

Footed Schoppen

English.

Pony English.

Schoppen Punty.

½ Schoppen Punty.

Pony Spanish.

Spanish.

Med. Delmonico Flared.

Large Delmonico. Flared.

Huber Footed.

Nº 128.

Large Delmonico.

Med. Delmonico.

London.

Pony London.

ALE GLASSES.

Scale ¼

BEER MUGS

12 Flute.

Pony St. Louis.

Pony.

BERLIN MUGS. PAT.

Scale ¼

¼ st. Albion Soda.

Pony 8 Flute.

Med. St. Louis.

Medium.

No. 1 Plain.

8 Flute

Large St. Louis.

Large

No. 1 Plain Cupped

Gesundheit

Gesundheit

Medium Pilsener

Large Stuck Handle

SODAS.

6 Flute.

Gut Heil.

Large Turner. Oval.

Large Kaiser Pat'd.

Medium Stuck Handle.

7 Flute.

Gut Heil.

Med. Turner. Oval.

Med. Kaiser Pat'd.

Large Pony Stuck Handle

½ Qt. Plain, Cupped

BEER MUGS

Short Flute.

Pony Kaiser Pat'd.

Small Pony Stuck Handle.

½ Qt. Plain

21

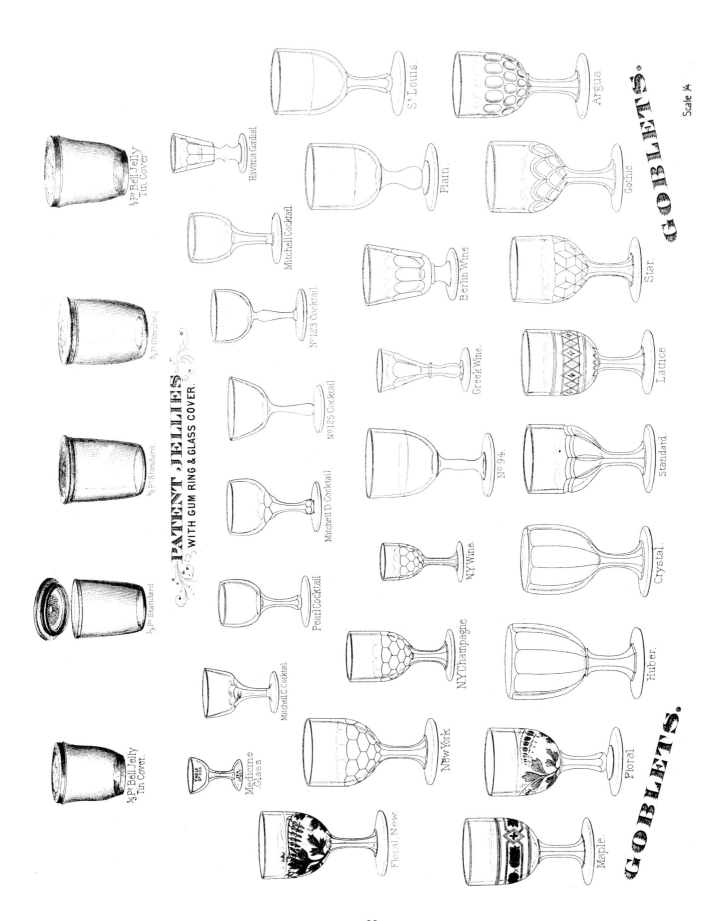

PATENT JELLIES
WITH GUM RING & GLASS COVER.

½ Pt Bell Jelly Tin Cover.

¾ Pt Standard

½ Pt Standard

⅓ Pt Standard

⅓ Pt Bell Jelly Tin Cover.

Havana Cordial.

Mitchell Cocktail.

Nº 123 Cocktail.

Nº 125 Cocktail.

Mitchell D Cocktail.

Pearl Cocktail.

Mitchell C Cocktail.

Medicine Glass

St Louis.

Plain.

Berlin Wine.

Greek Wine.

Nº 94.

N.Y. Wine.

N.Y. Champagne

New York

Floral New.

Argus.

Gothic.

Star.

Lattice

Standard.

Crystal.

Huber.

Floral.

Maple.

GOBLETS.

GOBLETS.

GOBLETS.

Scale ¼

22

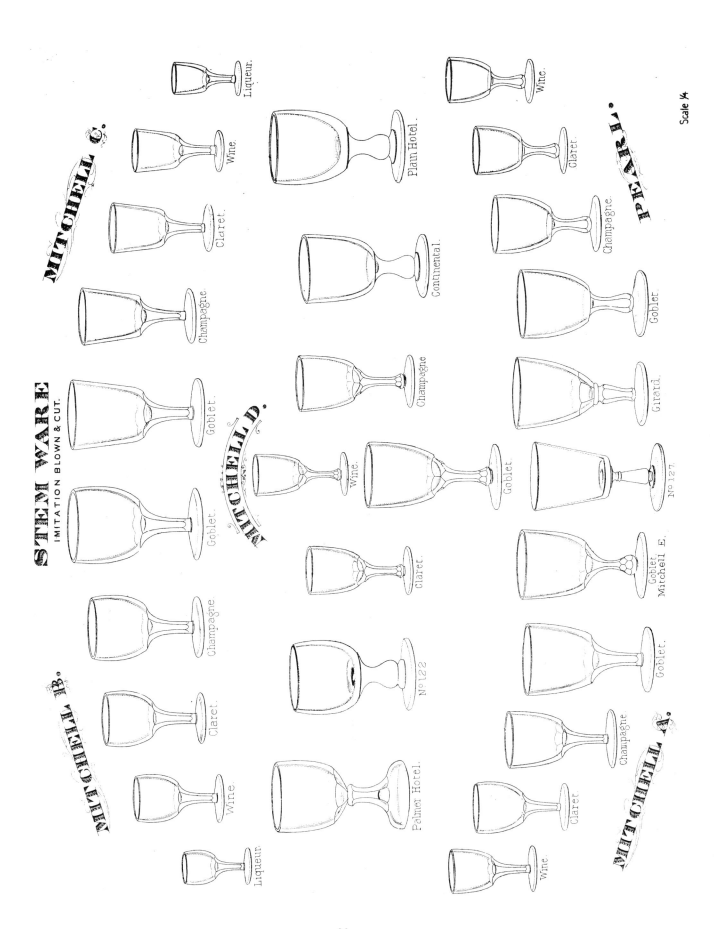

STEM WARE

IMITATION BLOWN & CUT.

MITCHELL C.

Liqueur.

Wine.

Claret.

Champagne.

Goblet.

Goblet.

Champagne.

Claret.

Wine.

Liqueur.

MITCHELL B.

Plain Hotel.

Continental.

Champagne.

Wine.

Claret.

No. 122

Palmer Hotel.

MITCHELL D.

Wine.

Goblet.

Goblet.

Wine.

Claret.

Champagne.

Goblet.

Girard.

No. 127

Goblet.
Mitchell E.

Goblet.

Champagne.

Claret.

Wine.

MITCHELL A.

PEARL.

Scale ¼

23

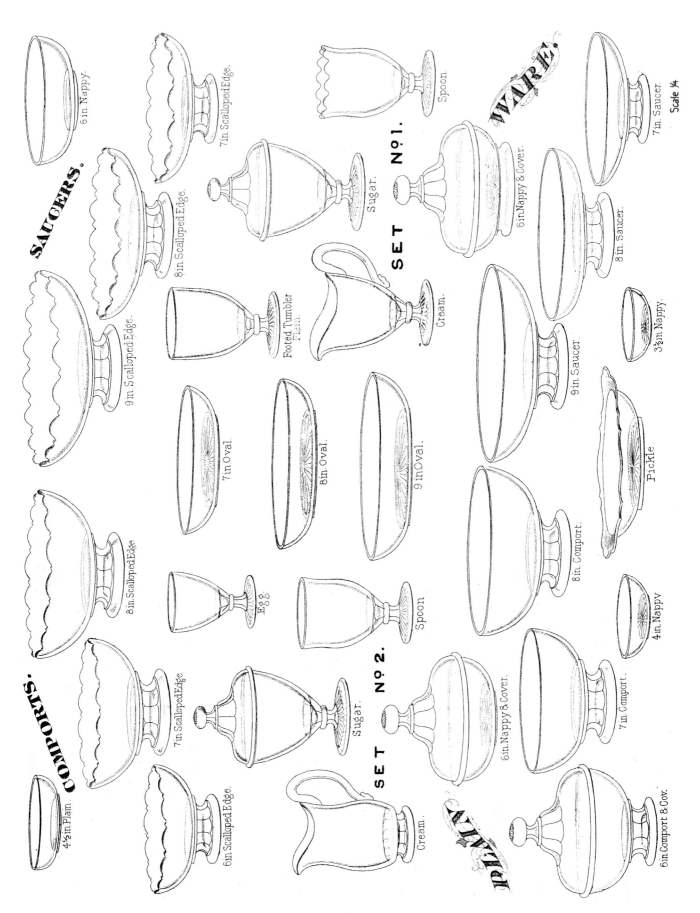

SAUCERS.

6 in. Nappy.

7 in. Scalloped Edge.

8 in. Scalloped Edge.

9 in. Scalloped Edge.

COMPORTS.

8 in. Scalloped Edge.

7 in. Scalloped Edge.

6 in. Scalloped Edge.

4½ in. Plain.

Spoon.

Sugar.

Footed Tumbler Plain.

Cream.

WARE.

SET Nº 1.

6 in. Nappy & Cover.

7 in. Saucer.

8 in. Saucer.

3½ in. Nappy.

9 in. Saucer

Pickle.

8 in. Comport.

4 in. Nappy

7 in. Oval.

8 in. Oval.

9 in Oval.

Egg.

Spoon.

Sugar.

SET Nº 2.

Cream.

PLAIN.

6 in. Nappy & Cover.

7 in. Comport.

6 in. Comport & Cov.

Scale ¼

24

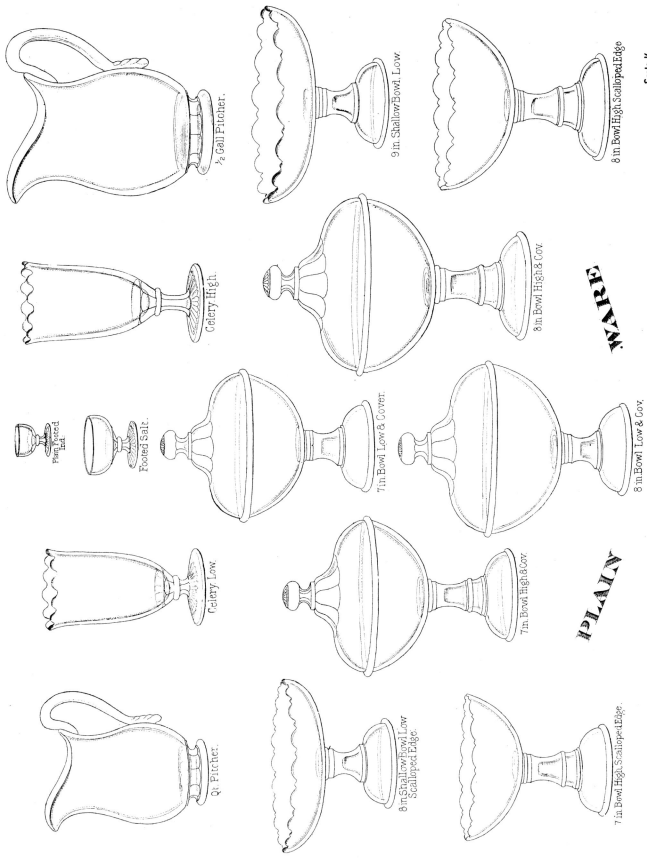

½ Gall Pitcher.

9 in. Shallow Bowl, Low.

8 in. Bowl High. Scalloped Edge.

Scale ¼

Celery. High.

8 in. Bowl High & Cov.

WARE.

Plain Footed Ind.

Footed Salt.

7 in. Bowl Low & Cover.

8 in. Bowl Low & Cov.

Celery. Low.

7 in. Bowl High & Cov.

PLAIN

Qt. Pitcher.

8 in. Shallow Bowl Low Scalloped Edge.

7 in. Bowl High. Scalloped Edge.

25

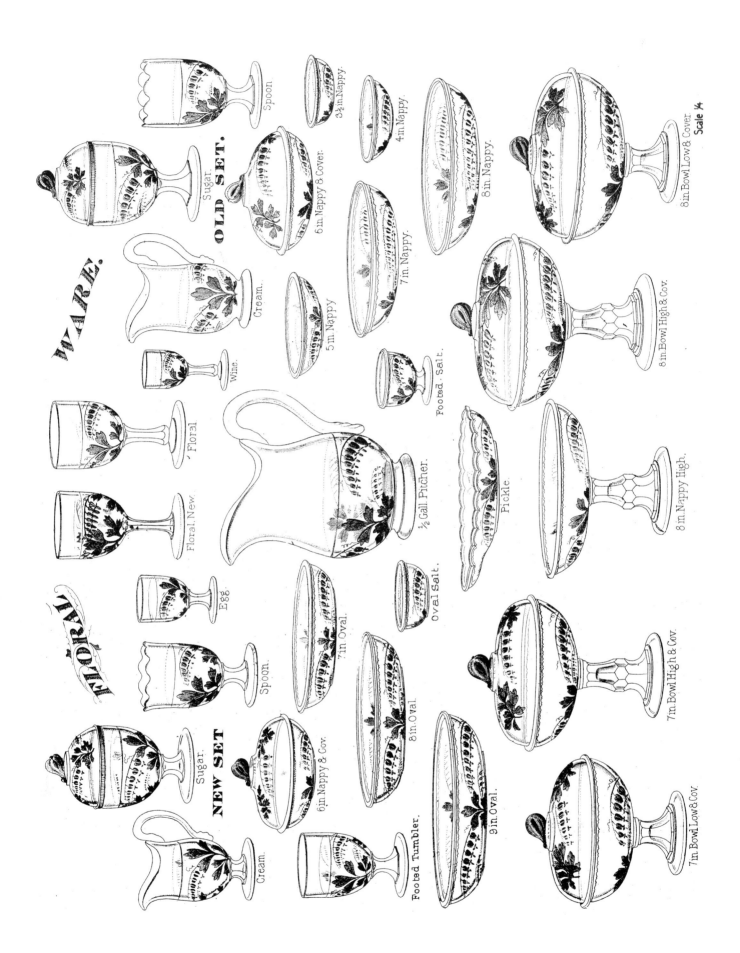

OLD SET.

WARE.

FLORAL

NEW SET.

Spoon

3½in.Nappy.

4in.Nappy.

8in.Nappy.

8in.Bowl.Low&Cover

Scale ¼

Sugar.

6in.Nappy&Cover.

7in.Nappy.

Cream.

5in.Nappy

Footed . Salt.

8in.Bowl.High&Cov.

Wine.

Floral

Floral.New.

½ Gall.Pitcher.

Pickle.

8in.Nappy.High.

Egg.

Spoon.

7in.Oval.

8in.Oval.

Oval.Salt.

7in.Bowl.High&Cov.

Sugar.

6in.Nappy&Cov.

9in.Oval.

Cream.

Footed.Tumbler.

7in.Bowl.Low&Cov.

26

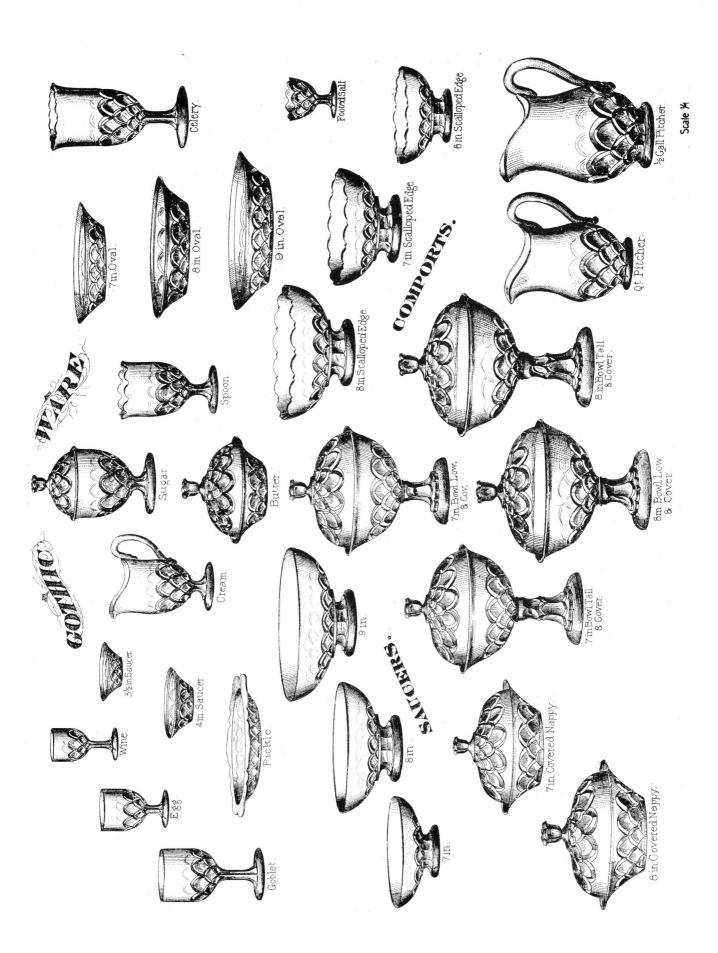

GOTHIC WARE

COMPORTS.

SAUCERS.

Celery.

Footd Salt

6 in. Scalloped Edge.

½ Gall. Pitcher.

Scale ¼

7 in. Oval.

8 in. Oval.

9 in. Oval.

7 in. Scalloped Edge.

Qt. Pitcher.

Spoon

8 in. Scalloped Edge.

8 in Bowl, Tall & Cover.

Sugar.

Butter.

7 in. Bowl, Low. & Cov.

8 in. Bowl, Low & Cover

Cream.

9 in.

7 in Bowl, Tall & Cover.

3½ in. Saucer.

4 in. Saucer.

Wine.

Pickle

8 in.

7 in. Covered Nappy.

Egg.

Goblet.

7 in.

8 in. Covered Nappy.

27

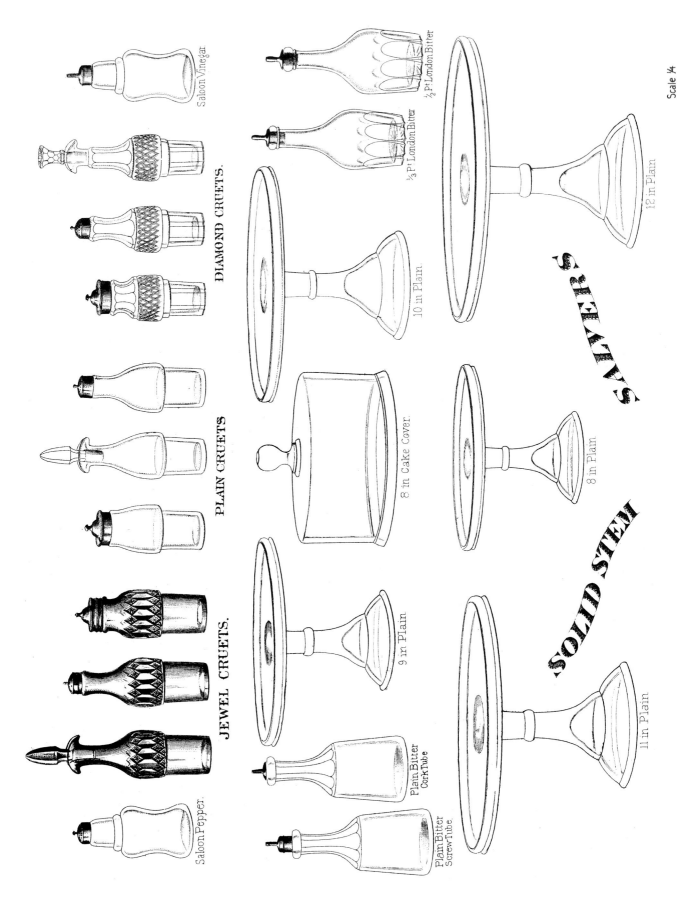

Saloon Vinegar.

DIAMOND CRUETS.

PLAIN CRUETS

JEWEL CRUETS.

Saloon Pepper.

½ Pt London Bitter

⅓ Pt London Bitter

10 in Plain.

8 in Cake Cover.

9 in Plain.

Plain Bitter Cork Tube.

Plain Bitter Screw Tube.

12 in Plain.

8 in Plain.

11 in Plain.

SALVERS

SOLID STEM

Scale ¼

SALTS.

Floral Footed
Pillar.
Plain Oval.
Plain Individ¹
Butter.

Ind. Shell
Salt
Argus Ind.
Plain Oval
Ind.

Diamond or
Cincinnati.
Brilliant Individ¹
Brilliant Salt

Diamond Ind.
Plain Round
Ind Pepper

Plain Footed
Ind.
Footed Salt
Plain.
"All Right"
Ind. Salt.

6 in. Nappy High & Cov.

Scale ¼

Cream.

Sugar

ARGUS SET.

6 in. Nappy Low & Cover.

Spoon.

SALTS.

Plain Square Ind.
Square Ind.
Fluted
Salt Duster.

Shell Salt.
Plain Square
Prism Individual
Royal Ind.
Royal.

Gem Ind.
Prism.

Maple Footed
Gem.
Floral Oval.

Standard Celery.

Celery or Spoon.

29

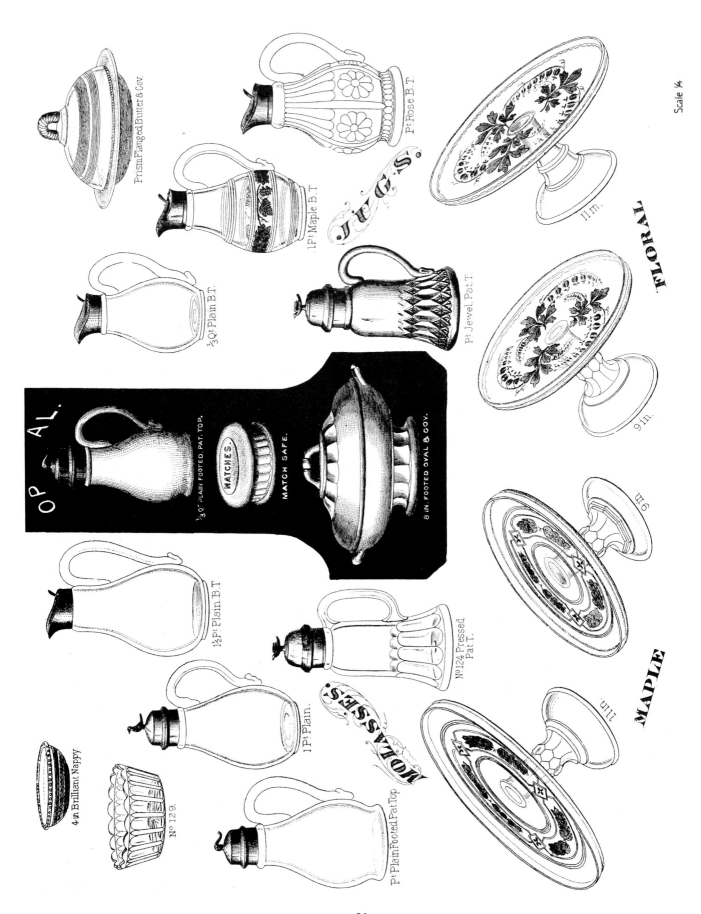

Prism Flanged Butter & Cov.

P.t Rose B.T

Scale ¼

JUGS.

1 P.t Maple B.T

FLORAL

11 in.

½ Q.t Plain B.T

P.t Jewel. Pat. T

9 in.

OP AL.

MATCHES.

MATCH SAFE.

½ Q.t Plain Footed Pat. Top.

8 IN. FOOTED OVAL & COV.

MAPLE

9 in.

N.º 124 Pressed Pat. T.

1½ P.t Plain. B.T

11 in.

4 in. Brilliant Nappy

N.º 129.

1 P.t Plain.

MOLASSES

P.t Plain Footed Pat Top

30

½ Pt

Pt.

1 Qt.

½ Gall.

¾ Gall.

1 Gall.

2 Gall.

1 Gall.

¾ Gall.

½ Gall.

Qt.

Pt.

Scale ¼

SQUAT AND TALL JARS

JAPANED TIN COVERS

31

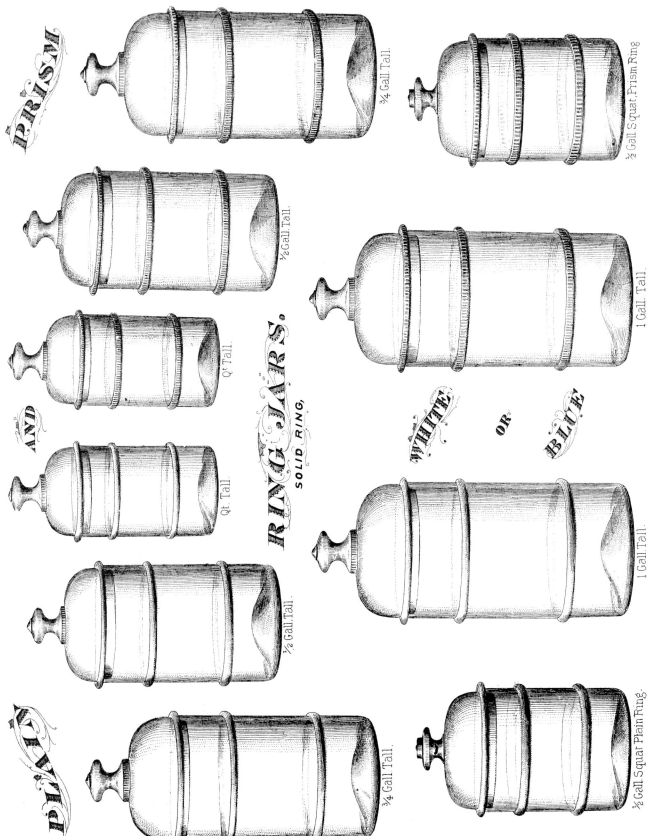

PRISM

PLAIN

AND

RING JARS,

SOLID RING,

WHITE OR BLUE

¾ Gall. Tall.

½ Gall. Tall.

Q.t Tall.

Q.t Tall.

½ Gall. Tall.

¾ Gall. Tall.

½ Gall. Squat, Prism Ring.

1 Gall. Tall.

1 Gall. Tall.

½ Gall. Squat Plain Ring.

Scale ¼

32

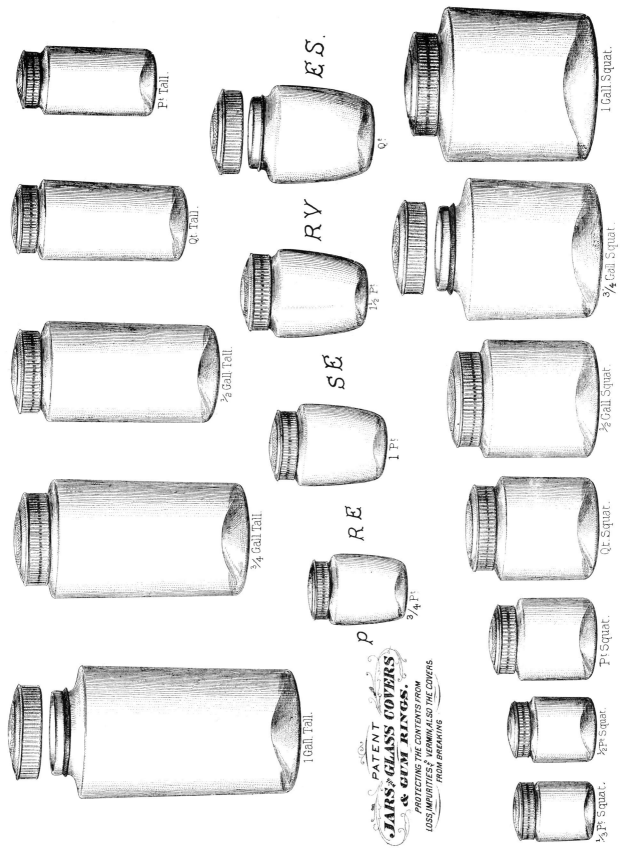

Pt. Tall.

Qt. Tall.

½ Gall. Tall.

¾ Gall. Tall.

1 Gall. Tall.

E S.

R Y

S E

R E

P

Q.t

1½ Pt.

1 Pt.

¾ Pt.

PATENT
JARS, GLASS COVERS
& GUM RINGS.

PROTECTING THE CONTENTS FROM
LOSS, IMPURITIES, & VERMIN, ALSO THE COVERS.
FROM BREAKING

1 Gall. Squat.

¾ Gall Squat.

½ Gall. Squat.

Qt. Squat.

Pt. Squat.

½ Pt. Squat.

⅓ Pt. Squat.

Scale ¼

33

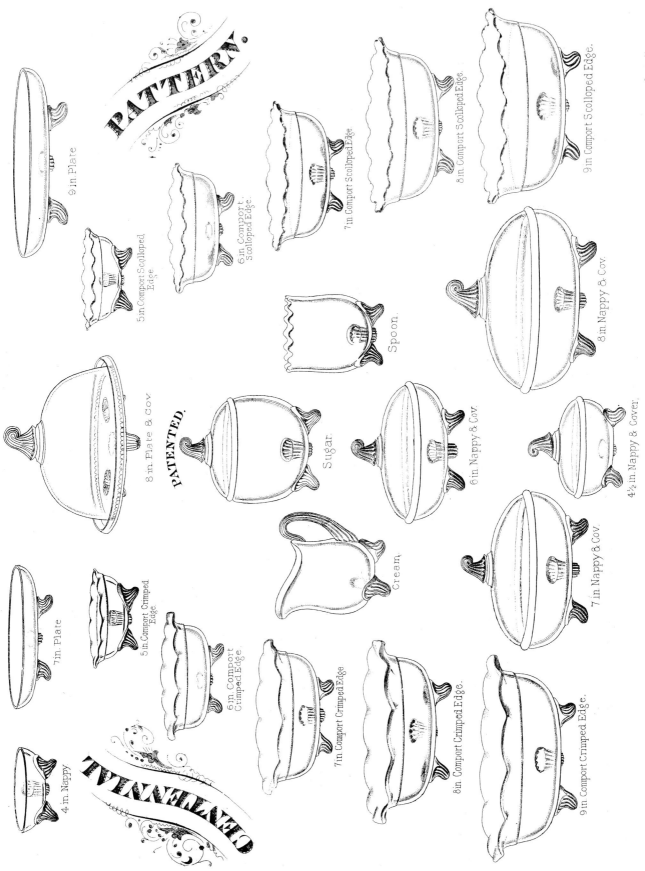

PATTERN.

9 in. Plate

5 in Comport Scolloped Edge.

6 in. Comport Scolloped Edge.

7 in Comport Scolloped Edge.

8 in Comport Scolloped Edge.

9 in Comport Scolloped Edge.

Scale ¼

Spoon.

8 in Nappy & Cov.

8 in. Plate & Cov.

PATENTED.

Sugar.

6 in. Nappy & Cov.

4½ in. Nappy & Cover.

Cream.

7 in Plate

5 in Comport Crimped Edge.

6 in. Comport Crimped Edge.

7 in Comport Crimped Edge.

8 in. Comport Crimped Edge.

7 in Nappy & Cov.

9 in Comport Crimped Edge.

4 in. Nappy

PATENTED.

34

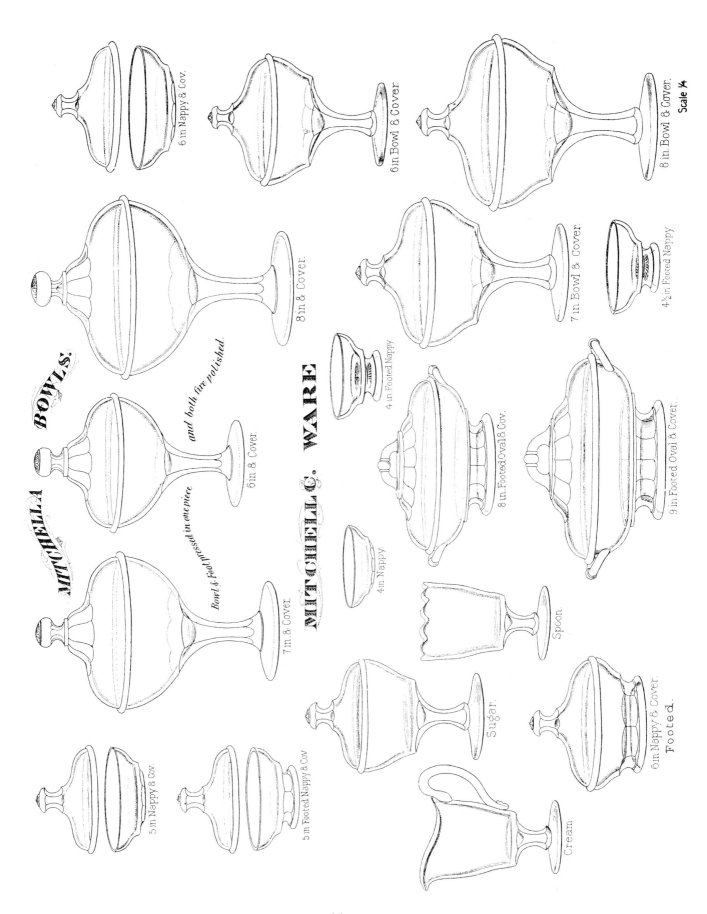

MITCHELL BOWLS.

MITCHELL & Co. WARE

6 in Nappy & Cov.

6 in Bowl & Cover

8 in Bowl & Cover.

Scale ¼

8 in & Cover.

7 in Bowl & Cover.

4½ in Footed Nappy

6 in & Cover.

Bowl & foot pressed in one piece and both fire polished.

7 in & Cover.

4 in Footed Nappy

4 in Nappy

8 in. Footed Oval & Cov.

9 in Footed Oval & Cover.

Spoon.

Sugar.

6 in Nappy & Cover. Footed.

Cream.

5 in Nappy & Cov.

5 in Footed Nappy & Cov

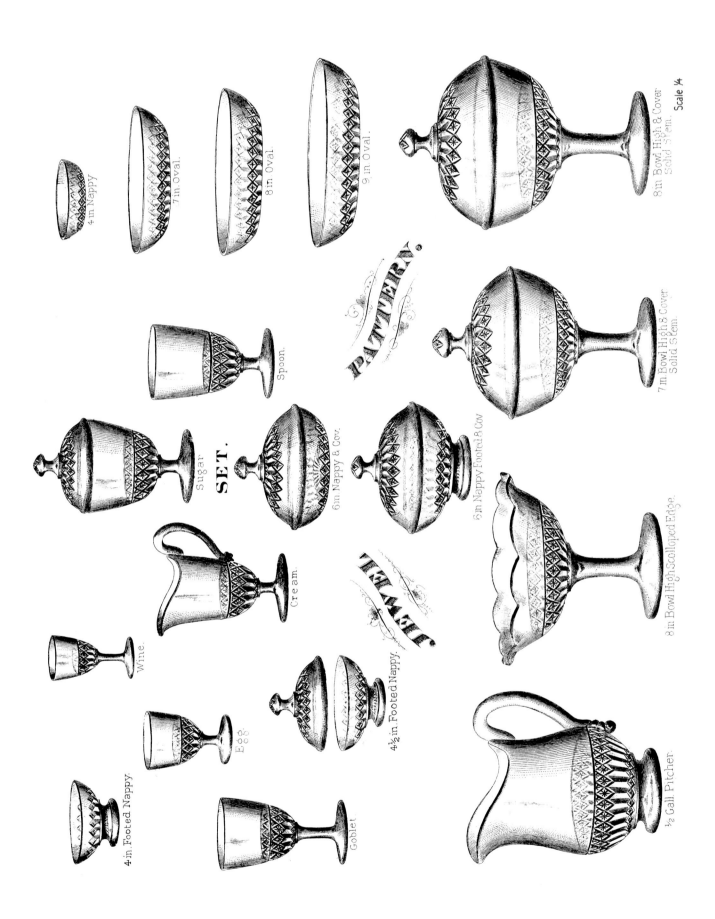

4 in Nappy

7 in. Oval.

8 in. Oval.

9. in Oval.

8 in. Bowl High & Cover Solid Stem.

Scale ¼

PATTERN.

Spoon.

7 in Bowl High & Cover Solid Stem.

Sugar

SET.

6 in Nappy & Cov.

6 in Nappy Footed & Cov

Cream.

JEWEL

8 in Bowl High Scalloped Edge.

Wine.

Egg.

4½ in. Footed Nappy.

4 in. Footed Nappy.

Goblet

½ Gall Pitcher.

36

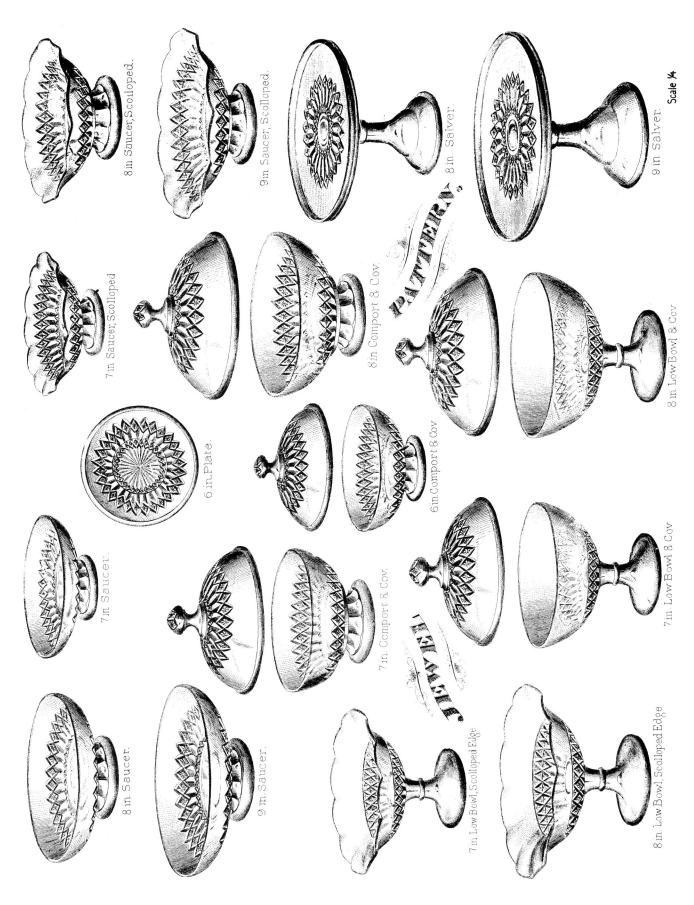

8 in. Saucer, Scolloped.

9 in. Saucer, Scolloped

9 in. Saucer, Scolloped.

8 in. Salver.

9 in. Salver.

Scale ¼

7 in. Saucer, Scolloped

8 in. Comport & Cov.

8 in. Low Bowl & Cov.

PATTERN.

6 in. Plate.

6 in. Comport & Cov.

7 in. Saucer.

7 in. Comport & Cov.

7 in. Low Bowl & Cov.

JEWEL

8 in. Saucer.

9 in. Saucer.

7 in. Low Bowl, Scolloped Edge

8 in. Low Bowl, Scolloped Edge

37

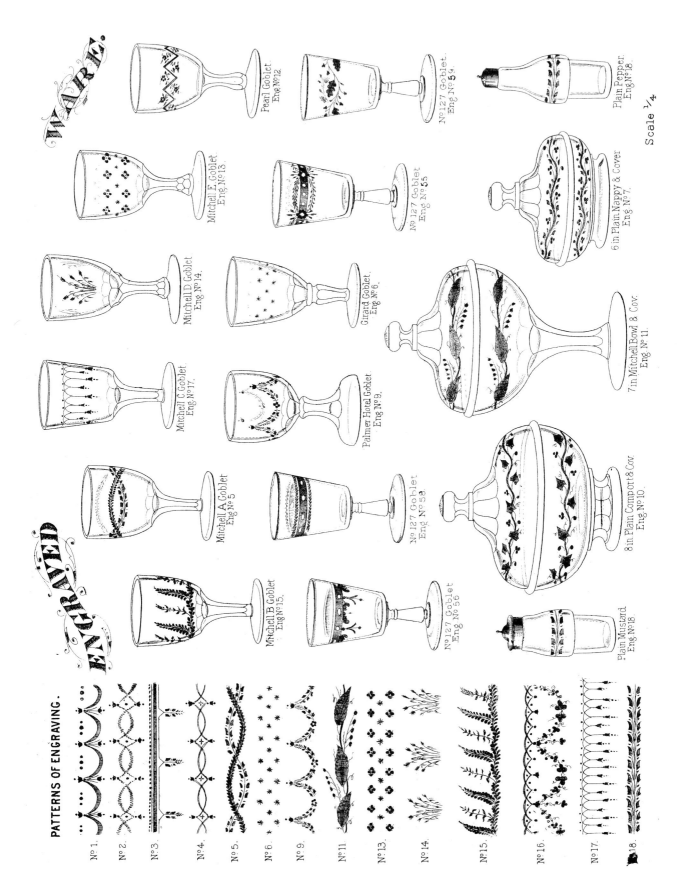

WARE.

Pearl Goblet. Eng. N°12.

N° 127 Goblet. Eng. N° 54.

Plain Pepper. Eng. N° 18.

Scale ¼

Mitchell E. Goblet Eng. N°13.

N° 127 Goblet Eng. N° 55.

6 in. Plain Nappy & Cover Eng. N° 7.

Mitchell D Goblet Eng. N° 14.

Girard Goblet. Eng. N° 6.

7 in. Mitchell Bowl & Cov. Eng. N° 11.

Mitchell C Goblet Eng. N° 17.

Palmer Hotel Goblet Eng. N° 9.

Mitchell A Goblet Eng. N° 5

N° 127 Goblet Eng. N° 58

8 in. Plain Comport & Cov. Eng. N° 10.

ENGRAVED

Mitchell B Goblet Eng. N° 15.

N° 127 Goblet Eng. N° 56

Plain Mustard Eng. N° 18.

PATTERNS OF ENGRAVING.

N° 1.
N° 2.
N° 3.
N° 4.
N° 5.
N° 6.
N° 9.
N° 11.
N° 13.
N° 14.
N° 15.
N° 16.
N° 17.
18.

38

Eng Nº 36.

Eng Nº 86.

Eng Nº 47.

Letter & Wreath.

Eng Nº 48.

Eng Nº 34.

Eng Nº 44.

Eng Nº 35.

Eng Nº 45.

Eng Nº 00.

O

K

P

S

L

U

M

J

N

Q

PATTERNS,
BY LETTERS.

FROSTED & CUT
DESIGNATED

39

Oval Pickle Jar

Mustard

7 in Oval

8 in Oval

9 in Oval

8 in. Bowl, Flared.

Scale ¼

Footed Salt & Cov.

Egg.

6 in. Bowl, Flared.

PATTERN.

Spoon.

½ Gallon Pitcher.

7 in. Bowl, Flared.

Sugar.

6 in Nappy & Cover.

Flange Butter.

Celery.

Nº 13

Cream.

7 in. Bowl, High & Cov.

Wine.

4 in Footed Nappy.

3 Pt Pitcher.

6 in Bowl & Cover, High.

Goblet.

4¼ in Footed Nappy.

4 in Nappy.

6 in Nappy.

Pickle Jar (Round).

8 in. Bowl, High & Cov.

40

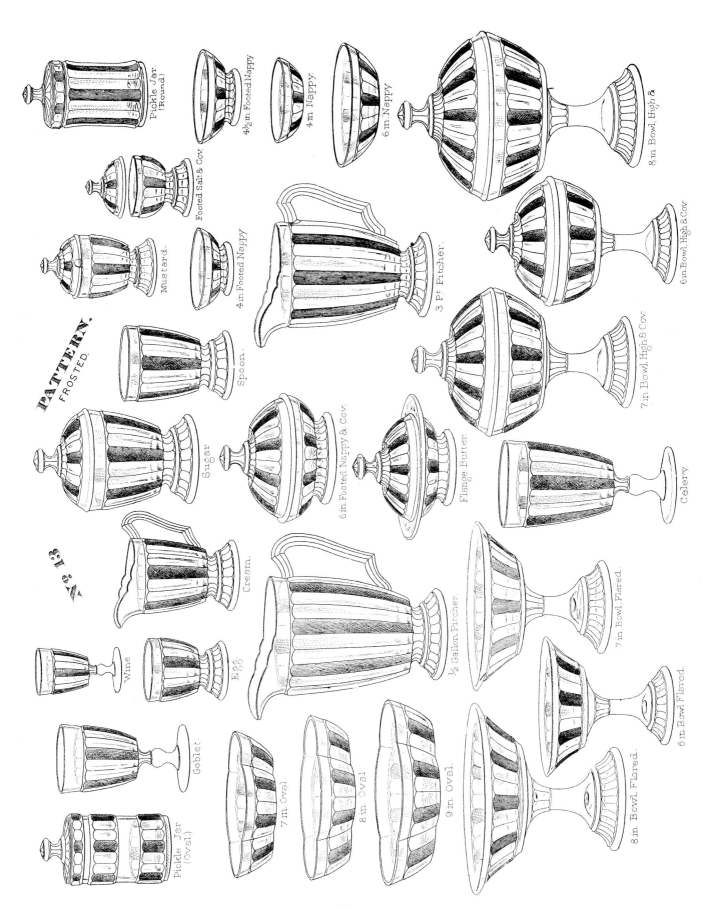

Pickle Jar (Round)

4½ in. Footed Nappy

4 in. Nappy.

6 in. Nappy

8 in. Bowl, High &

Footed Salt & Cov.

6 in. Bowl, High & Cov.

Mustard.

4 in. Footed Nappy

3 Pt. Pitcher.

7 in. Bowl, High & Cov.

PATTERN. FROSTED.

Spoon.

Sugar

6 in. Footed Nappy & Cov.

Flange Butter.

Celery

No. 13

Cream.

½ Gallon Pitcher.

7 in. Bowl, Flared.

Wine

Egg

6 in. Bowl Flared.

Goblet.

7 in. Oval.

8 in. Oval

9 in. Oval.

8 in. Bowl, Flared.

Pickle Jar (Oval)

41

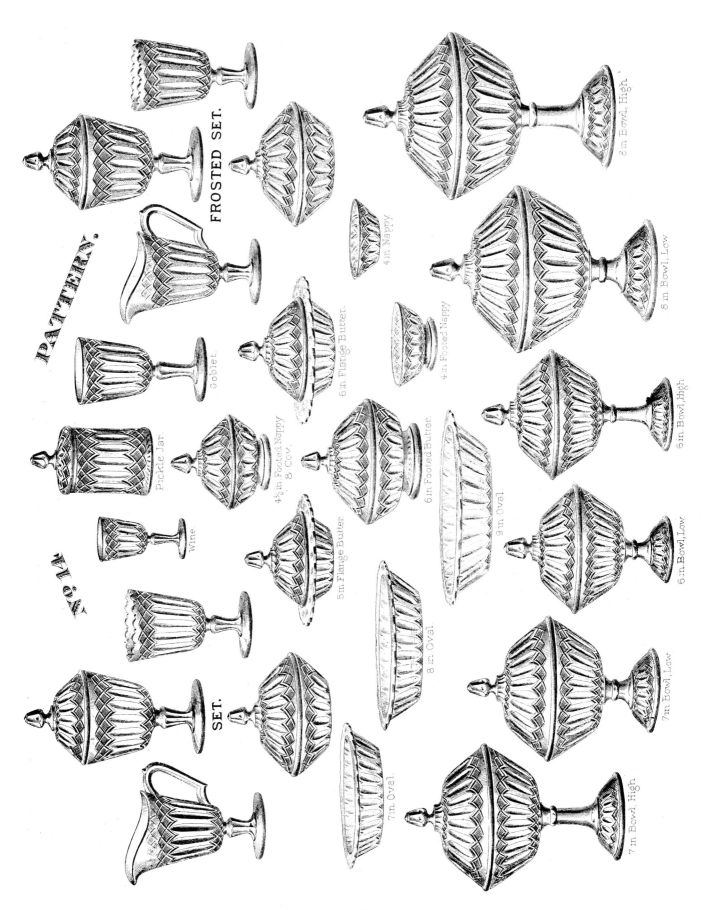

FROSTED SET.

PATTERN.

No 14

SET.

Goblet.

Pickle Jar.

Wine.

4 in. Nappy

4 in. Footed Nappy

6 in Flange Butter.

4½ in. Footed Nappy & Cov.

6 in Footed Butter.

5 in Flange Butter.

9 in. Oval.

8 in. Oval.

7 in. Oval.

8 in Bowl, High.

8 in Bowl, Low.

6 in Bowl, High.

6 in Bowl, Low.

7 in Bowl, Low.

7 in Bowl, High

42

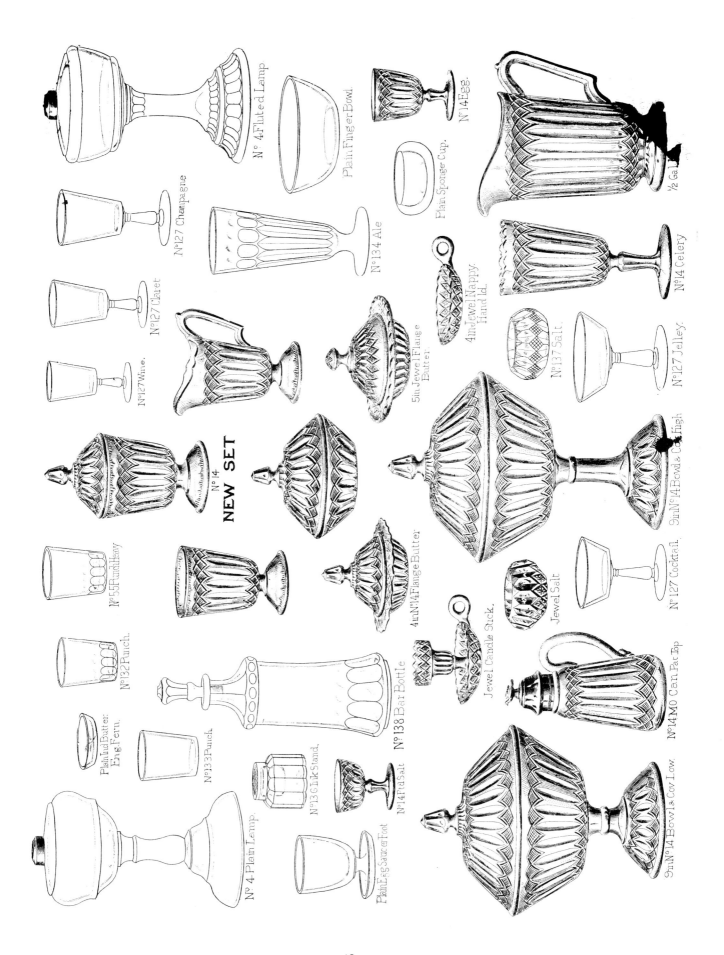

Nº 4 Fluted Lamp

Plain Finger Bowl

Nº 14 Egg.

Plain Sponge Cup.

½ Gal.

Nº 127 Champagne

Nº 134 Ale

Nº 14 Celery

Nº 127 Claret

4 in Jewel Nappy. Hand ld.

Nº 14 Bowl & Cov. High

Nº 127 Jelley.

Nº 127 Wine.

5 in Jewel Flange Butter.

Nº 137 Salt.

NEW SET

Nº 14

Nº 55 Punch Heavy.

4 in Nº 14 Flange Butter

Jewel Salt

9 in Nº 14 Bowl & Cov. High

Nº 127 Cocktail.

Nº 132 Punch.

Jewel Candle Stick.

Plain lined Butter: Eng. Fern.

Nº 138 Bar Bottle

Nº 14 MO Can. Pat. Top.

Nº 133 Punch.

Nº 13 G Ink Stand,

Nº 14 Ftd Salt.

Nº 4 Plain Lamp.

Plain Egg Saucer Foot

9 in Nº 14 Bowl & Cov. Low.

43

PEN PATTERN

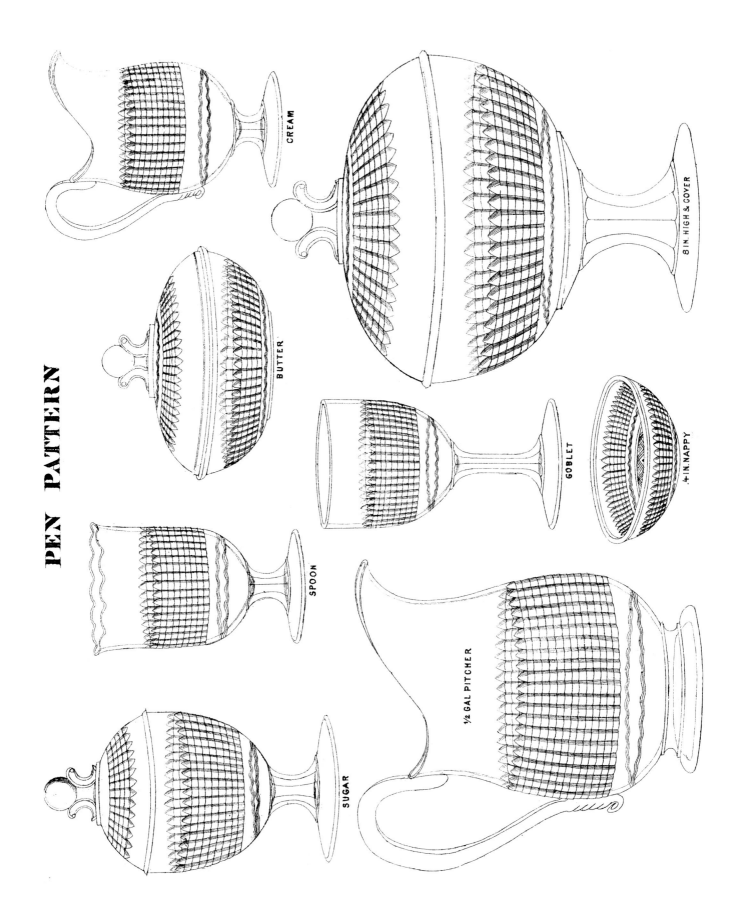

CREAM

8 IN. HIGH & COVER

BUTTER

GOBLET

4 IN. NAPPY

SPOON

½ GAL. PITCHER

SUGAR

44

THE PHOENIX GLASS COMPANY

The Phoenix Glass Company's 1893 catalog of gas and electric globes and other lighting fixtures was the fifth to be issued. Founded in 1880 by Andrew Howard, the firm was noted in the 80's for its fine colored cut glass. So great was the company's commercial success during these early years of the "Brilliant" period that capital was available to develop an even more lucrative line of etched and cut globes and shades.

An English etcher, Joseph Webb, was with the firm from 1887 to 1897 and was responsible for developing new designs and decorating methods. As the price lists accompanying the plates indicate, many items were not cheap goods, particularly those made of rich cut glass. Phoenix also produced quite elaborate hand-painted and stained shades, some costing several hundred dollars.

The company maintained its plant at Monaca, a small Ohio River town northwest of Pittsburgh. Sales offices and showrooms were located in Pittsburgh, Chicago and New York in 1893. A brilliantly lit exhibit of globes, domes, stalactites, balls, shades, bulbs and cylinders was assembled for Chicago's World's Columbian Exposition of 1893.

Plate No. 16 originally appeared in color, the only illustration so printed. The majority of the items are shown with a ruby stain, several in canary, and a few in blue. Plate numbers 5, 6, 9, 11, 13, 15, 17, 19, 21, 23, 25, 27, and 32 have been eliminated from this selection, as they contain items varying only slightly from those illustrated elsewhere.

WHITE ACID GAS AND ELECTRIC GLOBES, Etc.

Per Dozen.

3178.		
3179.	White Acid Squats, 7½ in. diam., 5 in. holder, . . .	$3.50
5721.		
5722.		
5723.		
3173.		
3176.		
4201.	White Acid Cones, 7½ in. diam., 4 in. holder ; 8 in. diam., 5 in. holder,	3.50
5725.		
5726.		
4204½.	White Acid Pan, 5¼ in. diam., 4 in. high, 2¼ in. holder, . . .	3.90
4204.	" " 8 " 4 " 4 " . .	4.20
5724½.	" Cone, 5 " 4 " 2¼ " . .	3.50
5724.	" " 7½ " 4 " 4 " .	3.50
5728½.	" Pan, 5¼ " 4 " 2¼ " .	3.90
5728.	" " 8 " 4 " 4 " .	4.20
5729½.	" " 5¼ " 4 " 2¼ " .	3.90
5729.	" " 8 " 4 " 4 " .	4.20
5730½.	" " 5¼ " 4 " 2¼ " .	3.90
5730.	" " 8 " 4 " 4 " .	4.20
5595.	Etched Crown, Masonic, 7½ in. and 8 in. diam., 4 in. and 5 in. holder,	14.00
3971.	" Rushton, Knights of Pythias, 7½ in. diam., 4 in. holder, .	8.00
3972.	" Squat, G. A. R., 7½ in. diam., 5 in. holder, .	6.00
100.	Ruby Lettered, Fire Escape, 7½ in. diam., 5 in holder, . .	15.00
101.	" Stairs, 7½ in. diam., 5 in. holder, . .	15.00

5723

5726

5730½

5730

STAIRS

101

5722

5725

5729½

5729

FIRE ESCAPE

100

5721

4201

5728½

5728

3972

3179

3176

5724½

5724

3971

3178

3173

4204½

4204

5505

47

Plate No. 2.

ETCHED SQUATS AND CROWNS.

3152.
3156.
3160.
3164.
4421.
4422.
4454.   Etched Squats, 7½ in. diam., 5 in. holder, ... $5.00   Per Dozen.
5105.
5709.
5710.
3125.
3131.
3133.
3134.
3136.
3137.
3138.
4424.   Etched Crowns, 7½ in. and 8 in. diam., 4 in. and 5 in. holder, $8.13
4456.
5705.
5117.
5153.
5706.
5707.
5731.

48

4421

5710

3136

5705

5781

3164

5709

3134

4456

5707

3160

5105

3138

4424

5706

3156

4454

3181

3138

5153

3152

4422

3125

3137

5117

49

ETCHED GAS and ELECTRIC PANS and CONES.

		Per Dozen.
4962½. Etched Pan, 5¼ in. diam., 4 in. high, 2¼ in. holder, . . .		$5.50
4962. " " 8 " 4 " 4 "		5.63
5588½. " " 5¼ " 4 " 2¼ "		5.50
5588. " " 8 " 4 " 4 "		5.63
5713½. " " 5¼ " 4 " 2¼ "		5.50
5713. " " 8 " 4 " 4 "		5.63
5714½. " " 5¼ " 4 " 2¼ "		5.50
5714. " " 8 " 4 " 4 "		5.63
5734½. " " 5¼ " 4 " 2¼ "		5.50
5734. " " 8 " 4 " 4 "		5.63

3143.
3145.
3150.
4460.
4461.   Etched Cones, 7½ in. or 8 in. diam., 4 in. and 5 in. holder, . $5.00
5115.
5116.
5711.
5712.
5733.

5665.
5666.   Etched, 7½ in. diam., 4¼ in. high, 4 in. holder, . . $7.00
5667.
5668.   Electrics to match, 4½ in. diam., 4⅜ in. high, 2¼ in. holder, .   6.25
5669.

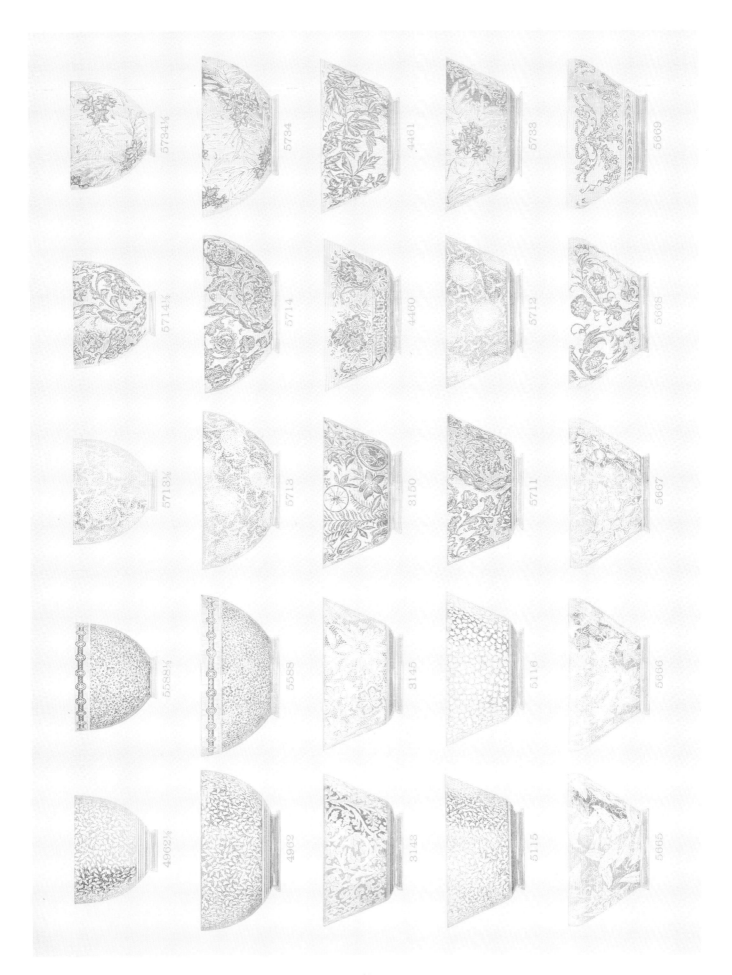

Plate No. 4.

ETCHED GAS AND ELECTRIC GLOBES.

	Description	diam.		high		holder	Per Dozen.
5740½.	Etched Pan, Scalloped Top,	5¼ in.	"	4 in.	"	2¼ in.	$7.00
5740.	"	8	"	4	"	4	7.50
5735½.	"	5¼	"	4	"	2¼	7.00
5735.	"	8	"	4	"	4	7.50
5739½.	"	5¼	"	4	"	2¼	7.00
5739.	"	8	"	4	"	4	7.50
5736½.	Cone,	5	"	4	"	2¼	6.25
5736.	"	7½	"	4	"	4	6.75
5737½.	"	5	"	4	"	2¼	6.25
5737.	"	7½	"	4	"	4	6.75
5751½.	Fluted Top,	6	"	3½	"	2¼	6.75
5751.	"	8	"	4½	"	4	8.00
5589½.	"	6	"	4	"	2¼	6.00
5589.	"	8	"	4¼	"	4	8.00
5337½.	Twist Rib,	5	"	4¼	"	2¼	6.00
5337.	"	7½	"	4¼	"	4	7.00
5559½.	Pressed, Scalloped Top,	5¼	"	4	"	2¼	3.00
5559.	"	7½	"	4	"	4	4.00
5349½.	Prism,	5¼	"	4	"	2¼	3.00
5349.	"	7½	"	4½	"	4	4.00

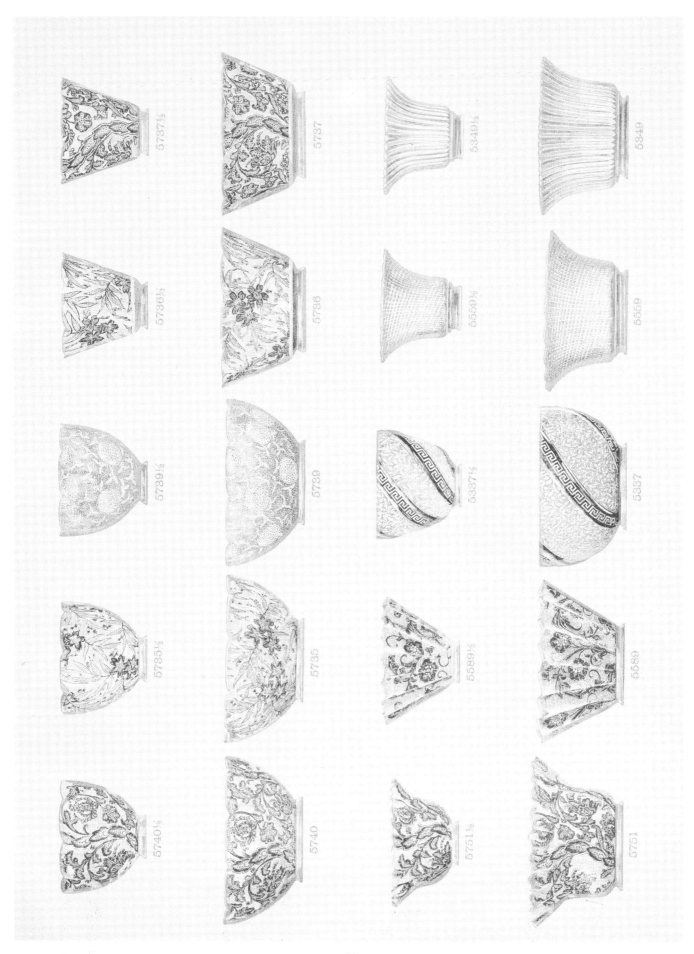

57371/2   5737   53491/2   5349

57361/2   5736   55591/2   5559

57391/2   5739   53371/2   5337

57351/2   5735   55891/2   5589

57401/2   5740   57511/2   5751

Plate No. Z.

"ELECTRO" ETCHED GAS AND ELECTRIC GLOBES.

		diam.	high	holder	Per Dozen.
5656½.	Etched Pan, Scalloped Top,	5¼ in.	4 in.	2¼ in. holder, .	$7.50
5656.	" " "	8 "	4 "	4 "	9.00
5629½.	" " "	5 "	4 "	2¼ "	7.50
5629.	" " "	7½ "	4 "	4 "	9.00
5703½.	" " "	5¼ "	4 "	2¼ "	10.00
5703.	" " "	8 "	4 "	4 "	12.50
5635½.	" " "	5 "	4 "	2¼ "	7.50
5635.	" " "	7½ "	4 "	4 "	9.00
5585½.	Melon Pan, Scalloped Top,	5¼ in.	4 in.	2¼ in. holder,	9.00
5585.	" " "	8 "	4 "	4 "	10.50
5792½.	" " "	5 "	4¼ "	2¼ "	13.00
5792.	" " "	7½ "	4¼ "	4 "	16.00
5794½.	" " "	6 "	3¼ "	2¼ "	13.00
5794.	" " "	7½ "	3¾ "	4 "	15.00
5793½.	" " "	5¼ "	4 "	2¼ "	9.00
5793.	" " "	8 "	4 "	4 "	10.50

54

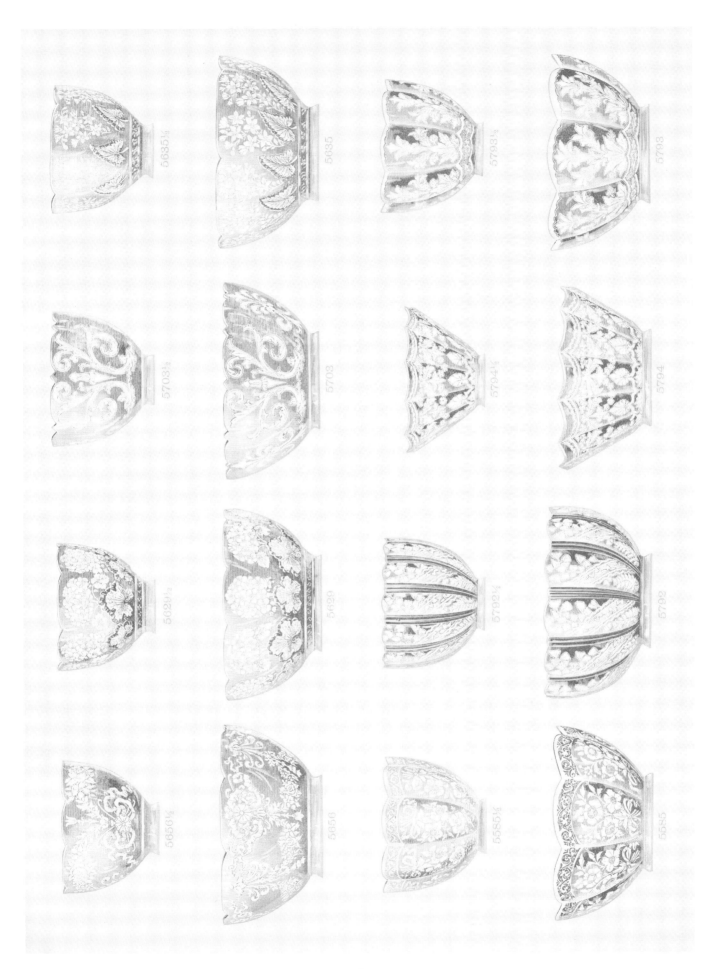

5635½

5635

5793½

5793

5703½

5703

5794½

5794

5620½

5620

5792½

5792

5656½

5650

5585½

5585

55

SILVER ETCHED GAS AND ELECTRIC GLOBES.

							Per Dozen.
5664½.	Silver Etched, Plain Top,	.	4¾ in. diam.,	4¼ in. high,	2¼ in. holder,	.	$17.00
5664.	" " "		7½ "	5¼ "	4 "	.	20.00
5296½.	" Beveled Edge,	.	5 "	4 "	2¼ "	.	15.00
5296.	" " "	.	7½ "	4 "	4 "	.	18.00
5220½.	" Scalloped Top,	.	5 "	3½ "	2¼ "	.	17.00
5220.	" " "	.	7½ "	3¾ "	4 "	.	20.00
5493½.	" Beveled Edge,	.	5¼ "	4 "	2¼ "	.	15.00
5493.	" " "	.	8 "	4 "	4 "	.	18.00
5797½.	" Melon, Scalloped Top,	.	4½ "	5 "	2¼ "	.	12.00
5797.	" " "	.	7½ "	5¼ "	4 "	.	20.00
5795½.	" Scalloped Top,	.	5 "	4 "	2¼ "	.	14.00
5795.	" " "	.	7½ "	4 "	4 "	.	16.00
5798½.	" Pan, Plain Top,	.	3¾ "	4 "	2¼ "	.	10.00
5798.	" " "	.	7¼ "	3¾ "	4 "	.	12.50
5796½.	" Crescent, Scalloped Top, 5		3½ "	2¼ "		.	15.00
5796.	" " "	.	7½ "	4 "	4 "	.	17.50

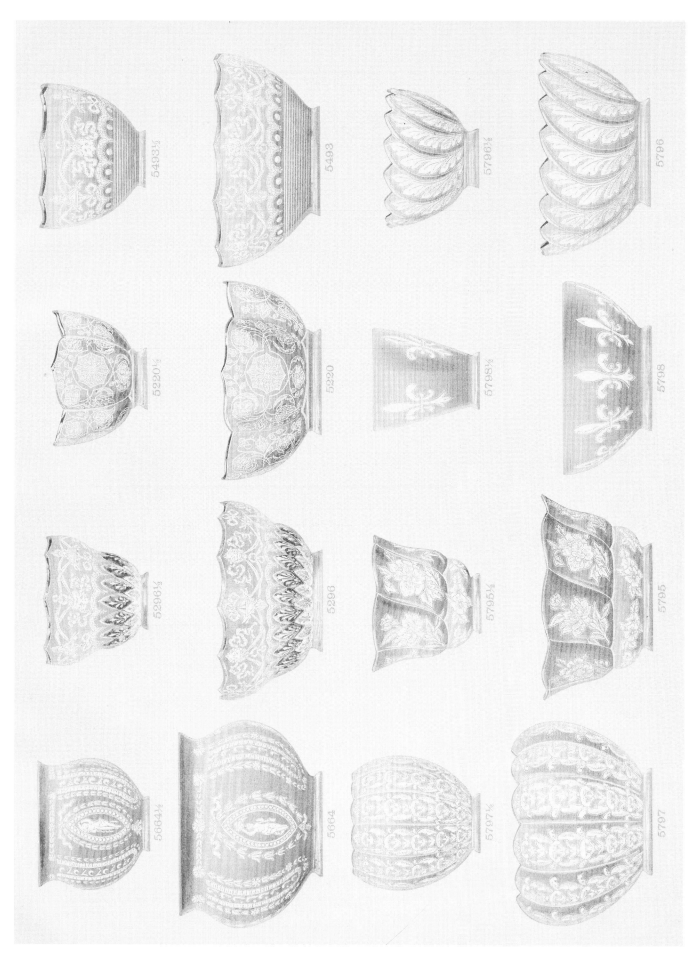

57

Plate No. 12.

RICH CUT GAS AND ELECTRIC GLOBES.

					Per Dozen.
5146½.	Rich Cut, Scalloped Top,	4⅛ in. diam.,	4½ in. high,	2¼ in. holder,	$50.00
5146.	"	7¾ "	4¾ "	4 "	88.00
5552½.	"	3¾ "	4¼ "	2¼ "	75.00
5552.	"	7½ "	4 "	4 "	90.00
3409½.	"	5 "	4¾ "	2¼ "	75.00
3409.	"	7½ "	4¼ "	4 "	90.00
5491½.	"	5 "	4 "	2¼ "	60.00
5491.	"	7½ "	4¾ "	4 "	70.00
5555½.	"	4½ "	4¼ "	2¼ "	48.00
5555.	"	7½ "	4 "	4 "	58.00
5762½.	"	5 "	4 "	2¼ "	50.00
5762.	"	7½ "	4 "	4 "	60.00
5139½.	"	5 "	4 "	2¼ "	50.00
5139.	"	7½ "	4 "	4 "	60.00
5496½.	"	4¼ "	4¼ "	2¼ "	30.00
5496.	"	7½ "	4½ "	4 "	46.00

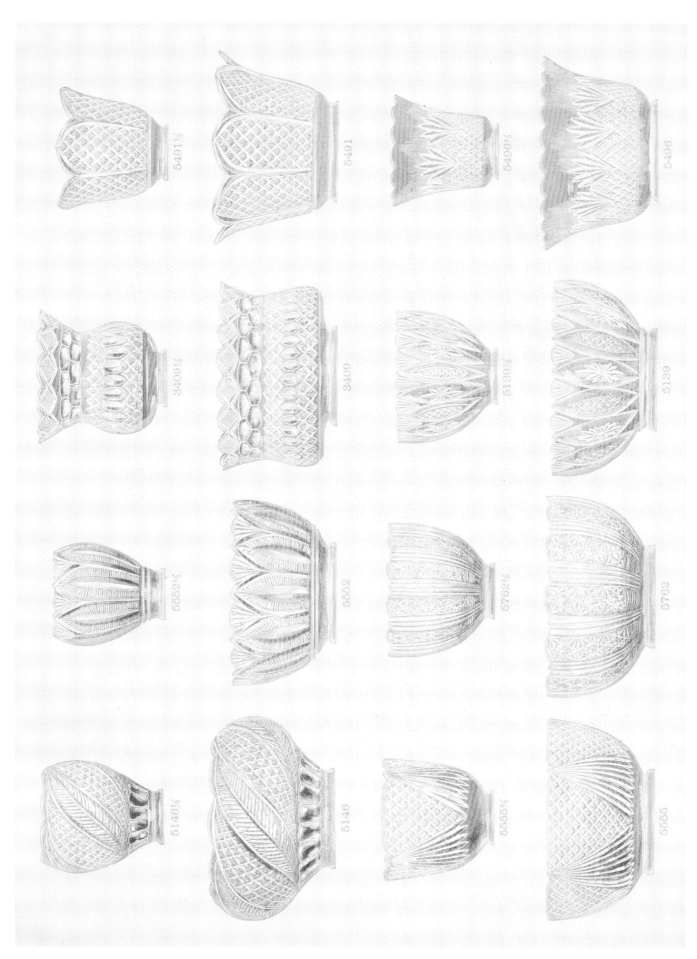

5491½

5491

5496½

5496

3409½

3409

5189½

5189

5552½

5552

5762½

5762

5146½

5146

5555½

5555

59

Plate No. 16.

COLORED ETCHED GAS AND ELECTRIC GLOBES, CANDLES AND BOBECHES.

No.	Description		diam.		high		holder		Per Dozen.
3288½.	Etched Crystal, with Rose, Blue, Orange and Citron Tinted Edges,	5½	in. diam.,	4¾	in. high,	2¼	in. holder,		$15.00
	All Crystal, not Tinted Edges,	5½	"	4¾	"	2¼	"		12.00
3288.	Etched Crystal, with Rose, Blue, Orange and Citron Tinted Edges,	8	"	5½	"	4	"		24.00
	All Crystal, not Tinted Edges,	8	"	5½	"	4	"		15.00
5110½.	Etched, Pink Opalescent and Ruby,	5	"	3½	"	2¼	"		24.00
	" Flint Opalescent, Light Blue Opalescent or Amber,	5	"	3½	"	2¼	"		20.00
	" Crystal,	5	"	3½	"	2¼	"		15.00
5110.	" Pink Opalescent and Ruby,	7½	"	4	"	4	"		30.00
	" Flint Opalescent, Light Blue Opalescent or Amber,	7½	"	4	"	4	"		24.00
	" Crystal,	7½	"	4	"	4	"		17.50
5109½.	" Pink Opalescent and Ruby,	5	"	3¾	"	2¼	"		24.00
	" Flint Opalescent, Light Blue Opalescent or Amber,	5	"	3¾	"	2¼	"		20.00
	" Crystal,	5	"	3¾	"	2¼	"		15.00
5109.	" Pink Opalescent and Ruby,	7½	"	4	"	4	"		30.00
	" Flint Opalescent, Light Blue Opalescent or Amber,	7½	"	4	"	4	"		24.00
	" Crystal,	7½	"	4	"	4	"		17.50
5635½.	" Pink Opalescent and Ruby,	5	"	4	"	2¼	"		18.00
	" Flint Opalescent, Light Blue Opalescent or Amber,	5	"	4	"	2¼	"		15.00
	" Crystal,	5	"	4	"	2¼	"		7.50
5635.	" Pink Opalescent and Ruby,	7½	"	4	"	4	"		22.50
	" Flint Opalescent, Light Blue Opalescent or Amber,	7½	"	4	"	4	"		17.50
	" Crystal,	7½	"	4	"	4	"		9.00
4570½.	" Pink Opalescent and Ruby,	6	"	4½	"	2¼	"		15.00
	" Flint Opalescent, Light Blue Opalescent or Amber,	6	"	4½	"	2¼	"		11.00
	" Crystal,	6	"	4½	"	2¼	"		6.00
4570.	" Pink Opalescent and Ruby,	8	"	4	"	4	"		18.00
	" Flint Opalescent, Light Blue Opalescent or Amber,	8	"	4	"	4	"		14.00
	" Crystal,	8	"	4	"	4	"		8.00
5541.	Stalactite, Venetian Thread, Assorted Colors,	4¾	"	6¼	"	3¼	"		24.00
5282½.	Electric Shade, Venetian Thread, Assorted Colors,	5	"	4	"	2¼	"		15.00
4177½.	Etched Crystal, with Rose, Blue, Orange and Citron Tinted Edges,	6	"	4½	"	2¼	"		14.00
	" All Crystal, not Tinted Edges,	6	"	4½	"	2¼	"		10.00
4176½.	" Crystal, with Rose, Blue, Orange and Citron Tinted Edges,	7	"	4	"	2¼	"		17.50
	" All Crystal, not Tinted Edges,	7	"	4	"	2¼	"		12.50
4175½.	" Crystal, with Rose, Blue, Orange and Citron Tinted Edges,	7	"	4	"	2¼	"		20.00
	" All Crystal, not Tinted Edges,	7	"	4	"	2¼	"		14.00

No.	Description	diam.			Ruby.	Ivory.	Turquoise Blue.	Opal.
					Per Dozen.			
5323.	Bobeche, Fine Ribbed,	3¾	in. diam.,		$3.50	$2.00	$2.00	$1.60
5495.	" Corrugated Twist,	3	"		3.00	1.50	1.50	1.25
5437.	" Fluted,	3½	"		3.00	1.50	1.50	1.25
1005.	" Crimped, Crystal Edges,	4	"		7.00	3.75	3.75	3.00
5427.	" Ribbed,	3¼	"		3.00	1.50	1.50	1.25
5428.	" Ribbed, Scalloped Edges,	3½	"		3.50	2.00	2.00	1.60

No.	Description	diam.		length		Ruby.	Ivory.	Turquoise Blue.	Opal.
						Per Gross.			
92.	Candles, Twist,	1¼	in. diam.,	4 in. length,		$30.00	$17.50	$17.50	$15.00
90.	" Plain or Twist,	1¼	"	4 "		30.00	17.50	17.50	15.00
518.	" Twist,	1⅛	"	3 or 4 in. length,		30.00	17.50	17.50	15.00
	" "	1⅛	"	5 in. length,		30.00	17.50	17.50	15.00
	" "	1⅛	"	6 "		30.00	17.50	17.50	15.00
93.	" "	⅞	"	3 "		30.00	17.50	17.50	10.50
	" "	⅞	"	3½ "		30.00	17.50	17.50	12.00
	" "	⅞	"	4 "		30.00	17.50	17.50	13.50
	" "	⅞	"	5 "		30.00	17.50	17.50	15.00
	" "	⅞	"	6 "		30.00	17.50	17.50	15.00
91.	" Plain,	⅞	"	3 "		30.00	17.50	17.50	10.50
	" "	⅞	"	3½ "		30.00	17.50	17.50	12.00
	" "	⅞	"	4 "		30.00	17.50	17.50	13.50
	" "	⅞	"	5 "		30.00	17.50	17.50	15.00
	" "	⅞	"	6 "		30.00	17.50	17.50	15.00
5274.	" Fine Ribbed,	1	"	4 "		30.00	19.00	19.00	16.50
	" " "	1	"	5 "		30.00	19.00	19.00	16.50
5494.	" Plain, with Corrugated Bulb,	⅞	"	4½ "		30.00	22.50	22.50	19.00

60

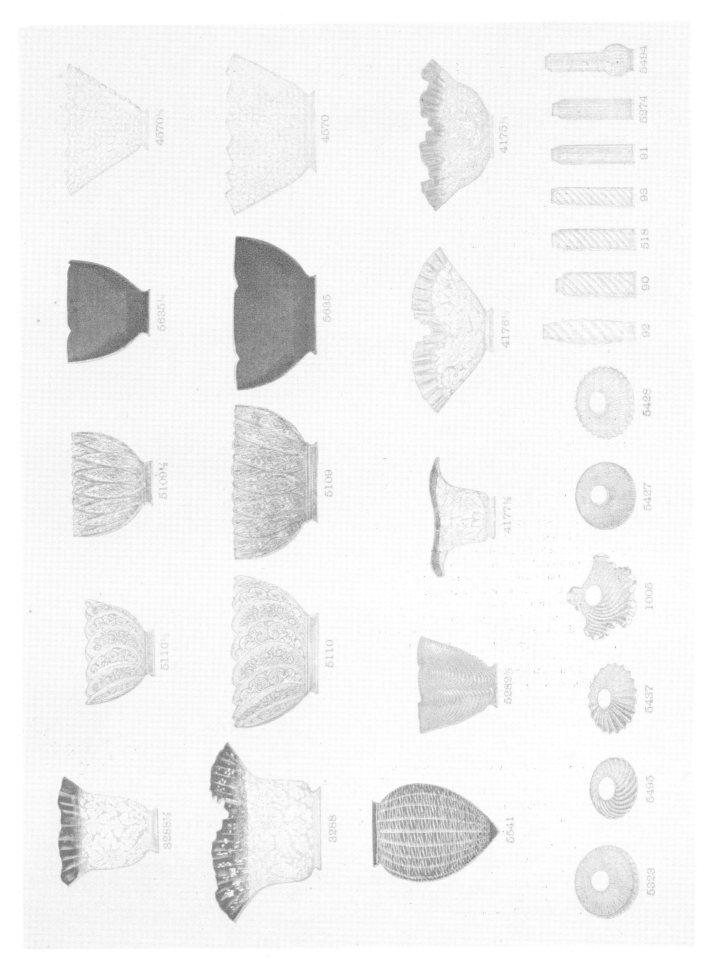

4570½

4570

4175½

5494

5274

91

93

518

90

92

5685½

5685

4176½

5429

5109½

5109

4177½

5427

5110½

5110

1005

5282½

5437

3288½

3288

5341

5495

5323

COLORED ELECTRIC GLOBES, SHADES, SMOKE BELLS, ETC.

No.	Description	Diam.	High	Holder	Per Dozen.
381.	Twist, Ruby or Pink Opalescent,	6 in. diam.,	5¼ in. high,	2¼ in. holder,	$9.00
	Flint Opalescent, Light Blue Opalescent or Amber,	6 "	5¼ "	2¼ "	5.00
1020.	Twist, Ruby or Pink Opalescent,	5½ "	4¼ "	2¼ "	9.00
	Flint Opalescent, Light Blue Opalescent or Amber,	5½ "	4¼ "	2¼ "	4.50
161½.	Twist, Ruby or Pink Opalescent,	5½ "	4¼ "	2¼ "	8.75
	Flint Opalescent, Light Blue Opalescent or Amber,	5½ "	4¼ "	2¼ "	4.38
4976.	Twist, Ruby or Pink Opalescent,	4¼ "	4¾ "	2¼ "	10.00
	Flint Opalescent, Light Blue Opalescent or Amber,	4¼ "	4¾ "	2¼ "	6.00
4975.	Twist, Ruby or Pink Opalescent,	5 "	5 "	2¼ "	10.00
	Flint Opalescent, Light Blue Opalescent or Amber,	5 "	5 "	2¼ "	6.00
4688.	Twist, Ruby or Pink Opalescent,	6¼ "	4 "	2¼ "	10.00
	Flint Opalescent, Light Blue Opalescent or Amber,	6¼ "	4 "	2¼ "	5.00
4569.	Twist, Melon, Ruby or Pink Opalescent,	4½ "	5 "	2¼ "	7.50
	Flint Opalescent, Light Blue Opalescent or Amber,	4½ "	5 "	2¼ "	3.50
1000.	Spot, Ruby or Pink Opalescent,	5 "	4¼ "	2¼ "	8.75
	Flint Opalescent, Light Blue Opalescent or Amber,	5 "	4¼ "	2¼ "	4.38
1003.	Diamond, Ruby or Pink Opalescent,	5 "	4 "	2¼ "	8.75
	Flint Opalescent, Light Blue Opalescent or Amber,	5 "	4 "	2¼ "	4.38
501.	Wart, Assorted Tinted Edges,	5½ "	4 "	2¼ "	12.00
158.	Spot, Ruby or Pink Opalescent,	5½ "	4 "	2¼ "	8.75
	Flint Opalescent, Light Blue Opalescent or Amber,	5½ "	4 "	2¼ "	4.38
4920.	Twist, Flint Opalescent,	5 in. diam.,	3¾ in. high,	2¼ in. holder or Edison Socket,	4.38
	Ruby,	5 "	3¾ "	2¼ " " "	8.75
4920.	Twist, Flint Opalescent,	6 "	3¾ "	2¼ " " "	4.65
	Ruby,	6 "	3¾ "	2¼ " " "	9.00
4920.	Twist, Flint Opalescent,	7 "	3¾ "	2¼ " " "	4.90
	Ruby,	7 "	3¾ "	2¼ " " "	9.25
5213.	Flint Opalescent,	6 "	3¼ "	2¼ " " "	4.50
	Opal,	6 "	3¼ "	2¼ " " "	2.50
5212.	Flint Opalescent,	5 "	2¼ "	2¼ " " "	4.25
	Opal,	5 "	2¼ "	2¼ " " "	2.25
4159.	Ribbed, Flint Opalescent, Assorted Tinted Edges,	7 in. diam.,	4 in. high,	2¼ in. holder,	15.00
	Flint Opalescent, not Tinted Edges,	7 "	4 "	2¼ "	7.00
4161.	Flint Opalescent, Assorted Tinted Edges,	7 "	4 "	2¼ "	14.00
	Flint Opalescent, not Tinted Edges,	7 "	4 "	2¼ "	7.00
3986.	Flint Opalescent, Assorted Tinted Edges,	6 "	4 "	2¼ "	12.00
	Flint Opalescent, not Tinted Edges,	6 "	4 "	2¼ "	6.50
4901.	Ribbed, Flint Opalescent,	5 "	4¼ "	2¼ "	6.25
4689.	Twist, Ruby or Pink Opalescent,	5 "	4¼ "	2¼ "	12.50
	Flint Opalescent, Light Blue Opalescent or Amber,	5 "	4¼ "	2¼ "	6.00
5778.	Ribbed, Crimped Top, Flint Opalescent,	6 "	6 "	2¼ "	7.50
4568.	Twist, Ruby,	6¼ "	4 "	2¼ "	10.00
	Flint Opalescent,	6¼ "	4 "	2¼ "	3.75
3779.	Spot, Flint Opalescent	6 "	2¼ "	2¼ "	5.00
	" "	7 "	2¼ "	2¼ "	5.50
	" "	8 "	2¼ "	2¼ "	6.00
	Crystal,	6 "	2¼ "	2¼ "	4.50
	"	7 "	2¼ "	2¼ "	5.00
	"	8 "	2¼ "	2¼ "	5.50

No.	Description	4 in.	5 in.	6 in.	7 in.	8 in.
12.	Smoke Bells, Etched Crystal, Assorted Patterns— Per dozen,	$5.50	$6.50	$8.00		
13.	" " Twist, Spot or Wart—					
	Ruby or Pink Opalescent,	8.00	9.25	10.00		
	Flint Opalescent, Light Blue Opalescent or Amber,	4.25	5.00	6.25		
14.	Smoke Shades, Twist, Spot or Wart—					
	Ruby or Pink Opalescent,		8.00	9.25	$10.00	$11.00
	Flint Opalescent, Light Blue Opalescent or Amber,		4.25	5.00	6.25	7.50
15.	Smoke Bells, Roughed,	2.50	2.88	3.25	3.50	
	" " Opal,	2.38	2.75	3.13	3.38	
	" " Clear,	2.25	2.50	3.00	3.25	
16.	Smoke Shades, Roughed,		2.75	3.00	3.13	3.50
	" " Opal,		2.50	2.75	2.88	3.25
	" " Clear,		2.38	2.63	2.75	3.13

4569
5212
4568
16

4688
5213
5778
15

4975
4920
4689
14

4976
158
4901
13

161½
501
3986
3779

1020
1003
4161
12

381
1000
4159

63

Plate No. 22.

SILVER ETCHED STALACTITES AND BALLS.

								Per Dozen.
5254.	Silver Etched Stalactite, Rich Cut Star Bottom, 5 in. diam., 6½ in. length, 3¼ in. holder,						.	$20.00
5662.	" " "	4¼	"	8¼	"	3¼	"	24.00
5571.	" " "	6½	"	9	"	5	"	42.00
5598.	" " "	4¼	"	6½	"	3¼	"	20.00
5301.	" and Rich Cut Stalactite,	5	"	6½	"	3¼	"	30.00

5636.	" Ball,	6 in.	7 in.	8 in.	10 in.	12 in.	14 in.	16 in.
	Per dozen,	$26.00	$32.00	$38.00	$54.00	$84.00	$120.00	$175.00

5636.	" Ball, Rich Cut Star Bottom—							
		6 in.	7 in.	8 in.	10 in.	12 in.	14 in.	16 in.
	Per dozen,	$30.00	$40.00	$45.00	$60.00	$90.00	$135.00	$225.00

| 5583. | " Stalactite, 9 in diam., 11 in. length, 4 in. or 5 in. holder, per dozen, | | | | | | . | $45.00 |

5637.	" Ball,	6 in.	7 in.	8 in.	10 in.	12 in.	14 in.	16 in.
	Per dozen,	$26.00	$32.00	$38.00	$54.00	$84.00	$120.00	$175.00

5637.	" Rich Cut Star Bottom—							
		6 in.	7 in.	8 in.	10 in.	12 in.	14 in.	16 in.
	Per dozen,	$30.00	$40.00	$45.00	$60.00	$90.00	$135.00	$225.00

65

SILVER ETCHED, ETCHED AND ROUGHED INSIDE BOWLS.

5806. Silver Etched Bowl, each, 12½ in., $11.00 ; 14 in., $15.00 ; 15 in., $17.50 ; 16 in., $27.50 ; 18 in., $42.00

5820. Etched Bowl, Rich Cut Star Bottom,   10 in.   12½ in.   14 in.   15 in.   16 in.   18 in.
Each, $10.00 $12.50 $16.00 $18.50 $30.00 $45.00

5821. Roughed Inside Bowl, Rich Cut Star Bottom,   10 in.   12½ in.   14 in.   15 in.   16 in.   18 in.   24 in.
Each, $10.00 $12.50 $16.00 $18.50 $30.00 $45.00 $62.50

5865. Etched Bowl, each, 10 in., $3.00 ; 12½ in., $5.50 ; 14 in., $9.00 ; 15 in., $13.00 ; 16 in., $20.00 ; 18 in., $30.00

5808. Silver Etched Bowl, 16 in. diam., 7¼ in. high, 10½ in. holder, ...   Each, $45.00

5866. "Electro" Etched Bowl, each, 10 in., $3.50 ; 12½ in., $6.00 ; 14 in., $10.00 ; 15 in., $14.50 ; 16 in., $22.00

5821

5866

5820

5808

5806

5865

67

Plate No. 26.

RICH CUT BALLS AND BOWLS.

5777. Rich Cut Ball, "Strawberry Diamond,"

	6 in.	7 in.	8 in.	10 in.	12 in.	14 in.	16 in.
Each,	$7.75	$8.75	$14.38	$31.25	$52.50	$75.00	$105.00

5819. Rich Cut Bowl, "Star and Hobnail," each, 10 in., $22.00; 12½ in., $37.50; 14 in., $54.00; 16 in., $75.00

5210. Rich Cut Ball, "Star and Hobnail,"

	6 in.	7 in.	8 in.	10 in.	12 in.	14 in.	16 in.
Each,	$8.12	$9.38	$16.75	$32.50	$56.25	$80.00	$112.50

5809. Rich Cut Ball, "Phœnix,"

	6 in.	7 in.	8 in.	10 in.	12 in.	14 in.
Each,	. .	$17.50	$22.50	$28.75	$45.00	$70.00	$100.00

5815. Rich Cut Bowl, "Jewel," . . Each, 10 in., $27.50; 12½ in., $45.00; 14 in., $60.00; 16 in., $90.00

5211. Rich Cut Ball, Heavy Rib, Beaded and Fan,

	6 in.	7 in.	8 in.	10 in.	12 in.	14 in.
Each,	$6.50	$7.00	$8.00	$14.00	$20.00	$30.00

THE AGNEW COMPANY, LTD.

The Agnew Company was a small manufacturer of utilitarian commercial glassware. The items it produced had been staples of American glasshouses since the eighteenth century. Flint glassware had been made in the Pittsburgh glass district for many years by several dozen firms, including some of those that were merged to form the United States Glass Company in 1891. Agnew was not one of them.

The company was located in Hulton, then 12 miles north of Pittsburgh, and was a member of the industry's trade organization, the Western Flint Bottle Association. Presumably, unlike such giants in the field as Whitall, Tatum, the Agnew Company served the needs of bottlers, druggists and food processors in a relatively small geographical area. Just when and how the company was founded is not known.

ILLUSTRATED CATALOGUE

AND

PRICES CURRENT

OF

THE AGNEW CO., Limited,

MANUFACTURERS OF

Flint Glass Bottles.

———

OFFICE AND WORKS,

HULTON, PA.

Twelve Miles North of Pittsburgh, on the A. V. R. R.

———

PITTSBURGH:
DUQUESNE PRINTING AND PUBLISHING CO., 60 SECOND AVE.
1894.

PRICES CURRENT

ADOPTED BY THE

Western Flint Bottle Association,

A T

CINCINNATI, OHIO, AUG. 8th, 1888.

PLEASE NOTICE CHANGE IN PRICES.

No Charge for Packages.

Packages other than Regular Sizes, Charged Extra.

Payment required, in all cases, in funds equal in value to U. S. Treasury notes, or Exchange on New York or Pittsburgh.   In no case will we pay Exchange.

All bills not remitted for when due will be drawn for at sight with notice.

Particular care will be exercised to have our Ware properly packed and shipped in good order, and we will not be responsible for breakage after shipment, considering railroad and steamboat receipts sufficient evidence that the goods were shipped in good order.

Moulds furnished at a cost of from ten to fifty dollars each.

NOTICE.

No agent has authority to guarantee prices under any circumstances. All Discounts are subject to change without notice. No Additional Discount, on any pretense whatever, will be allowed after goods are shipped.

Agents are not allowed to collect money exeept on written order.

LETTERED MOULDS.

We have French Square, Flat Prescription, Philadelphia Oval; also, Shoo Fly, Picnic and Polo Flask Moulds prepared for the insertion of names without the expense of a new mould. These lettered plates will fit only our own moulds.

We will furnish the lettered plates at prices ranging from $4.00 to $5.00 each, according to size and amount of lettering. These prices are for a plain inscription, not exceeding 25 letters. Additional letters will be charged 10 cents each; and Mortars, Scales, Monograms, &c., from 40 cents to $1.00 each. Long inscriptions detract from the appearance of the bottles, and are not recommended.

Prices of Lettered Ware is higher than Unlettered. Quotations on specified quantities given when desired. We cannot engage to make exactly the number ordered; there will always be a few over or under the order.

STYLES OF FINISH.

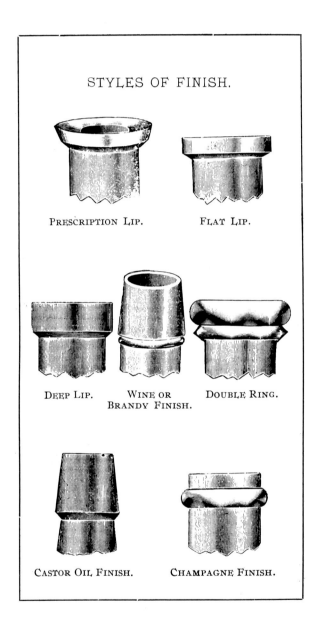

PRESCRIPTION LIP.   FLAT LIP.

DEEP LIP.   WINE OR   DOUBLE RING.
            BRANDY FINISH.

CASTOR OIL FINISH.   CHAMPAGNE FINISH.

SHOO FLY.

FLASKS.—Shoo Fly.

½ or 1 Gross Boxes,	Per gro.
¼ pt. 3 oz. capacity,	$10 00
½ pt. 5 & 6 oz. capacity,	12 00
1 pt. 10 & 12 oz. ..	19 00
1 qt. 24 oz. ..	30 00
½ pt. Full Measure -	15 00
1 pt. ...... -	22 00
1 qt. ...... - -	35 00

PICNIC.

FLASKS.—Picnic.

½ or 1 Gross Boxes.	Per gro.
¼ pt. 3 oz. capacity,	$10 00
½ pt. 4, 5 & 6 oz. capc'y,	12 00
1 pt. 8, 10 & 12 oz. ..	19 00
1 qt. 24 oz. ..	36 00

75

POLO.

FLASKS.—Polo.

½ or 1 Gross Boxes.		Per gro.
¼ pt. 3 oz. capacity,		$10 00
½ pt. 6 oz.	....	12 00
1 pt. 12 oz.	....	19 00
1 qt. 24 oz.	....	30 00

JO JO.

FLASKS.— Jo Jo.

½ or 1 Gross Boxes.		Per gro.
½ pt. 6 oz. capacity,		$12 00
1 pt. 12 oz.	....	19 00
1 qt. 24 oz.	....	30 00

76

UNION.

FLASKS.—Union.

½ or 1 Gross Boxes.	Per gro.
½ pt. 7 oz. capacity,	$12 00
1 pt. 14 oz. ...	19 00
1 qt. 28 oz.	30 00
½ pt. Full Measure,	15 00
1 pt.	22 00
1 qt.	35 00

NEWPORT.

FLASKS.—Newport.

½ or 1 Gross Boxes.	Per gro.
½ pt. 5 oz. capacity,	$12 00
1 pt. 10 oz.	19 00
1 qt. 23 oz.	30 00

PILLAR.

FLASKS.—Pillar.

½ or 1 Gross Boxes.	Per gro.
½ pt. 6 oz. capacity,	$12 00
1 pt. 12 oz.	19 00

COLUMBIAN.
Screw Top.

FLASKS.—Columbian.

SCREW TOP, WITH METAL CAP
AND CORK.

½ or 1 Gross Boxes.	Per gro.
½ pt. 6 oz. capacity,	——
1 pt. 12 oz.	——

OAKMONT.
Screw Top.

FLASKS —Oakmont.

SCREW TOP, WITH METAL CAP
AND CORK.

½ or 1 Gross Boxes.   Per gro.

½ pt. 6 oz. capacity,   ——

1 pt. 12 oz.   ....   ——

SHOO FLY.
Screw Top.

FLASKS.—Shoo Fly.

SCREW TOP, WITH METAL CAP
AND CORK.

½ or 1 Gross Boxes.   Per gro.

½ pt. 6 oz. capacity,   ——

·1 pt. 12 oz.   ....   ——

FRENCH SQUARE.   ROUND PRESCRIPTION,
                          or Packers.

FRENCH SQUARES.

8 oz.	1 Gross Boxes,	-		-	Per gross, $13 00
12 oz.	½	....	-	-	.... 19 00
16 oz.	½	....	-	-	.. 22 00
30 oz.	½	...	-	-	.... 35 00
32 oz.	½	,....	-	-	.... 35 00

ROUND PRESCRIPTION OR PACKERS.

8 oz.	1 Gross Boxes,		-		Per gross, $13 00
10 oz.	½	....	-	-	.... 17 00
12 oz.	½	....	-	-	.... 19 00
16 oz.	½	....	-	-	.... 22 00
20 oz.	½	..	-	-	.... 25 00
24 oz.	½	....	-	-	.... 28 00
30 oz.	½	....	-	-	.... 35 00
32 oz.	½	....	-	-	.... 35 00

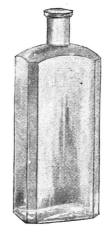

PHIL'A OVAL.   FLAT OR TALL BLAKE.

PHILADELPHIA OVALS.

8 oz.	1 Gross Boxes,	-	Per gross,	$13 00
16 oz.	½ ...	-	-	... 22 00
32 oz.	½	-	-	.... 35 00

FLAT PRESCRIPTION OR TALL BLAKES.

8 oz.	1 Gross Boxes,	-	Per gross,	$14 00
16 oz.	½	-	-	.... 23 00
32 oz.	½	-	-	.... 36 00

PITTSBURGH OVAL.   WASHINGTON OVAL.

PITTSBURGH OVALS.

8 oz.	1 Gross Boxes,	-	Per gross,	$14	00
16 oz.	½ ...	-	-	....	23 00
30 oz.	½ ...	-	-	....	36 00
32 oz.	½	-	-	....	36 00

WASHINGTON OVALS.

8 oz.	1 Gross Boxes,	-	Per gross,	$14	00
16 oz.	½	-	-	....	23 00
32 oz.	½	-	-	....	36 00

BRANDIES.

TALL BRANDY.   SQUAT BRANDY,
or Porter.

TALL BRANDIES.

8 to gall. ½ or 1 Gross Boxes,	-		Per gross, $26 00
6	......	-	-	.... 30 00
5	......	-		.... 32 00
4	......	-	-	.... 35 00

SQUAT, PLAIN.

8 to gall. ½ or 1 Gross Boxes,	-		Per gross, $26 00
5	......	-	-	.... 32 00
4	......	-		. .. 35 00

SQUAT BRANDY.
Seal.

BOSTON BRANDY.
Tall.

SQUAT BRANDIES.—Seal.

5 to gall. ½ or 1 Gross Boxes,   -   Per gross, $32 00
4 ....   - 35 00

BOSTON BRANDIES.—Tall.

5 to gall. ½ or 1 Gross Boxes,   -   Per gross, $32 00
4 ....   - 35 00

BOSTON BRANDY.
Squat.

FLUTED BRANDY.

BOSTON BRANDIES.—Squat.

5 to gall. ½ or 1 Gross Boxes, - Per gross, $32 00
4 .... - - 35 00

FLUTED BRANDIES.

5 to gall. ½ or 1 Gross Boxes, - Per gross, $32 00

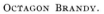

OCTAGON BRANDY.   HOCK WINE.

OCTAGON BRANDIES.

5 to gall. ½ or 1 Gross Boxes,   .   Per gross, $32 00

HOCK WINES.

6 to gall. ½ or 1 Gross Boxes,   -   Per gross, $30 00
5 ....   -   - 32 00

LIQUOR BOTTLES.

DECANTER.
No. 26.

TALL SEAL.
No. 33.

DECANTERS, No. 26.

5 to gall. ½ or 1 Gross Boxes, - Per gross, $32 00

TALL SEALS, No. 33.

30.00

6 to gall. ½ or 1 Gross Boxes, - Per gross, $~~28 00~~

5 .... - - 32 00

4 ... . - ... 35 00

BELLE OF BOURBON. TALL CORDIAL.

BELLE OF BOURBONS.

5 to gall. ½ or 1 Gross Boxes, - Per gross, $32 00
4 ....   -   - 35 00

TALL CORDIALS.

6 to gall. ½ to 1 Gross Boxes, - Per gross, $30 00

ROCK AND RYE.
No. 32.

ROCK AND RYE.
Ball Neck.
No. 34.

ROCK AND RYE, No. 32.

8 to gall. ½ or 1 Gross Boxes,		-		Per gross,	$26 00
6	......	-	-	....	30 00
5	......	-		....	32 00

ROCK AND RYE. B. N. No. 34.

6 to gall. ½ or 1 Gross Boxes, - Per gross, $30 00

No. 35.   Chartreuse.

No. 35.

5 to gall. ½ or 1 Gross Boxes,   -   Per gross, $32 00

CHARTREUSE.

8 to gall. ½ or 1 Gross Boxes,   .   Per gross, $26 00
4 ....   -   - 35 00

SQUAT SEAL.
No. 24.

SQUAT SEAL.
No. 25.

SQUAT SEAL.—No. 24.

5 to gall. ½ or 1 Gross Boxes,   -   Per gross, $32 00

SQUAT SEAL.—No. 25.

5 to gall. ½ or 1 Gross Boxes,   -   Per gross, $32 00

No. 39.   No. 75.

No. 39.

5 to gall. ½ or 1 Gross Boxes,   -   Per gross, $32 00

No. 75.

4 to gall. ½ or 1 Gross Boxes,   -   Per gross, $35 00

FRUIT BRANDY.   TAPER GIN.

FRUIT BRANDIES.

5 to gall. ½ or 1 Gross Boxes,   -   Per gross, $32 00

TAPER GINS.

6 to gall. ½ or 1 Gross Boxes,   -   Per gross, $30 00

MALT WHISKY.
Ball Neck.

MALT WHISKY.
Plain.

MALT WHISKEYS. –Plain.

5 to gall. ½ or 1 Gross Boxes,   -   Per gross, $32 00

MALT WHISKY.—Ball Neck.

5 to gall. ½ or 1 Gross Boxes,   -   Per gross, $32 00

FANCY BAR.
No. 77.

PANEL NECK BRANDY.

FANCY BAR, No. 77.

5 to gall. ½ or 1 Gross Boxes,   -   Per gross, $ ——

The above can be made with any of the following names blown in, viz.: Bourbon, Brandy, Blackberry, Rum, Rye, Gin, Whiskey, Port, Sherry, Kimmel.

PANELED NECK BRANDY.

5 to gall. ½ or 1 Gross Boxes,   -   Per gross, $32 00

GLOBE BITTER.
12 oz.

BITTER.
11 oz.

GLOBE BITTER.—12 OZ.

12 oz. 1 Gross Boxes,   -   - Per gross, $20 00

BITTER.—1 OZ.

11 oz. 1 Gross Boxes,   -   Per gross, $20 00

CHOW CHOW.

CHOW CHOW.
Fluted Shoulder.

CHOW CHOW.

½ pt. packed in casks or boxes,   -   Per gross, ——
1 pt.   ....   -   -   .. .   ——

CHOW CHOW.—Fluted Shoulder.

1 pt. packed in casks or boxes,   -   Per gross, ——

CHAMPAGNE CATSUP.   DECANTER CATSUP.

CHAMPAGNE CATSUP.

½ pt. packed in boxes or casks,   -   Per gross, ——
1 pt.   ....   -   -   ....   ——

DECANTER CATSUP.

½ pt. packed in boxes or casks,   -   Per gross, ——
1 pt   ....   -   -   ....   ——

RIBBED CATSUP.　　　　　CATSUP.
　　　　　　　　　　　　　Fluted Shoulder.

RIBBED CATSUP.

1 pt. in boxes or casks,　　　　　Per gross, ——

CAT&UP.—Fluted Shoulder.

½ pt. in boxes or casks,　　　　Per gross, ——
1 pt.　　....　　　　　　　　　....　——

AMERICAN PICKLE.　　　　RING PEPPER.

AMERICAN PICKLES.

½ pt. in boxes or casks,　　　-　Per gross, ——
1 pt.　　....　　　　-　　-　....　——

RING PEPPERS.

6 oz. in boxes or casks,　　　-　Per gross, ——

WORCESTERSHIRE SAUCE.

SALOON PEPPER.
6 oz.

SALOON PEPPER.
4 oz.

WORCESTERSHIRE SAUCE.

6 oz. in boxes or casks,   -   Per gross, ——

SALOON PEPPERS.—Wlthout Tops.

4 oz. in 1 Gross Boxes,   -   Per gross, ——
6 oz.   . . . .   -   - ·   . . . .   ——

MUSTARD,
No. 86.

IMPERIAL
Mustard.

BARRELL
Mustard.

MUSTARD, No. 86.

6 oz. per gross,   - - - - $12 00
8 ......   - - - - 14 00

IMPERIAL MUSTARD.

6 oz. per gross,   - - - - 12 00
8 ......   - - - - 14 00
16 ......   - - - - 23 00

BARRELL MUSTARD.

4 oz. per gross,   - - - - $10 00
6 ......   - - - - 12 00

FLINT GLASS BEER BOTTLES.

These Bottles are made in Flint Glass, and for private use and hotels, where a nice bottle is desired. They are a great improvement over the green glass bottle. We can furnish them either with or without stoppers. If desired name and address, can be blown on the bottle at a cost of from Five to Ten Dollars for each size name plate.

1 pint, per gross,   -   -   -   - $ ——
1 quart, ... -   -   -   -   -   ——

FLINT GLASS MILK BOTTLES.

These bottles are made extra heavy, fitted with the most approved stoppers, and lettered as shown in cut. If desired, name and address can be blown in each bottle. Cost of name plates from Five to Ten Dollars for each size bottle, and to be paid for when completed. Orders for lettered bottles must be for not less than five gross of either size. There will always be a few over or under the order which must be accepted in lieu of order given. Samples of either size will be sent on receipt of 25 cents.

Pints in 1 Gross Boxes, per Gross,   - $ ——
Quarts ½ ....   -   -   ——

AGNEW'S IMPROVED STANDARD FRUIT
JAR—FLINT GLASS.

This jar is made of the same thickness of glass throughout, and will stand the heating and filling much better than the old style standard jar.

Quarts, 8 doz. boxes, per Gross - - $ ——
½ Gallon, 6 doz. boxes, per Gross, - - ——

MASON FRUIT JAR—FLINT GLASS.

We furnish these jars complete or bodies only.

Pints 8 doz. boxes complete per gross,	-	$ ——
" 8	Bodies only per gross,	——
Quarts, 8	Complete, ...	-	——
" 8	Bodies only, ...	——
½ Gall. 6	Complete, ...	-	——
" 6	Bodies only, ...	——

T. B. CLARK & CO.

T. B. Clark & Co.'s "American Cut Glass" catalog of 1896, here presented in its entirety, is a find for any cut glass collector. Although not of the superb quality of Dorflinger and T. G. Hawkes, the Clark wares were very good, as is evident even in the illustrations following.

Thomas Byron Clark founded the firm in 1884 in Honesdale, Wayne County, not far from Dorflinger's White Mills plant. First employed by the Meriden Flint Glass Co., Clark was not a cutter but certainly knew his business. The firm was first known as Hatch and Clark, then briefly as Clark and Wood (Walter Wood, a brother-in-law), and by 1886 as T. B. Clark & Co. In 1895 Clark and Walter Wood established the Wayne Silver Company in Honesdale to produce silver fittings for their cut glass pieces. Few of these decorative pieces show up in the 1896 catalog.

The first Clark factory was built in Seelyville, near Honesdale, and later a second was set up in Hawley, also near by. A sales office and showroom was maintained in New York City. The trademark used until 1898 employed a picture of a cut glass carafe and the words "Clark & Co." above it. After 1898 a leaf-shaped trademark was employed. The name "Clark" was sometimes etched in script.

The "X" marks in a few of the following illustrations are to be found in the original catalog and may have been made by a salesman to indicate that a particular item was being or had been dropped from production.

T. B. CLARK & COMPANY'S AMERICAN CUT GLASS.

ROUND PUNCH BOWL, DESDEMONA.
14-inch, $48.00.

FOOTED PUNCH BOWL, CORAL.
14-inch, $90.00.
12 " 72.00.

FOOTED PUNCH BOWL, DESDEMONA.
14-inch, $90.00.
12 " 72.00.

DEEP PUNCH BOWL, DESDEMONA.
12-inch, $44.00.

ROUND PUNCH BOWL, ARBUTUS.
14-inch, $48.00.

108

T. B. CLARK & COMPANY'S AMERICAN CUT GLASS.

No. 250. Bowl, Desdemona.
9-inch, $24.00.

No. 120. Bowl, Adonis.
$30.00.

No. 700. Bowl, Arbutus.

7-inch, $12.00.
8   "   14.00.
9   "   18.00.
10 "   22.00.

No. 460. Bowl, Adonis.
9-inch, $29.00.

No. 700. Bowl, Magnolia.

8-inch, $24.00.
9   "   32.00.
10 "   40.00.

No. 121. Bowl, Desdemona.
$34.00.

T. B. CLARK & COMPANY'S AMERICAN CUT GLASS.

ROUND BOWLS, DESDEMONA.

8-inch, $21.00.
9   "   24.00.
10   "   30.00.
12   "   36.00.

ROUND BOWLS, MANHATTAN.

7-inch, $ 8.00.
8   "   11.00.
9   "   14.00.
10   "   18.00.
12   "   25.00.

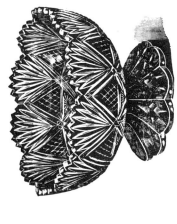

PRISCILLA BOWLS, MANHATTAN.

8-inch, $18.00.
9   "   21.00.

ROUND BOWLS, ARBUTUS.

8-inch, $14.00.
9   "   18.00.
10   "   22.00.

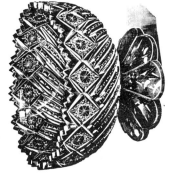

PRISCILLA BOWLS, ORIENT.

7-inch, $27.00.
8   "   33.00.
9   "   39.00.

ROUND BOWLS, VENUS.

8-inch, $16.00.
9   "   20.00.
10   "   24.00.
12   "   36.00.

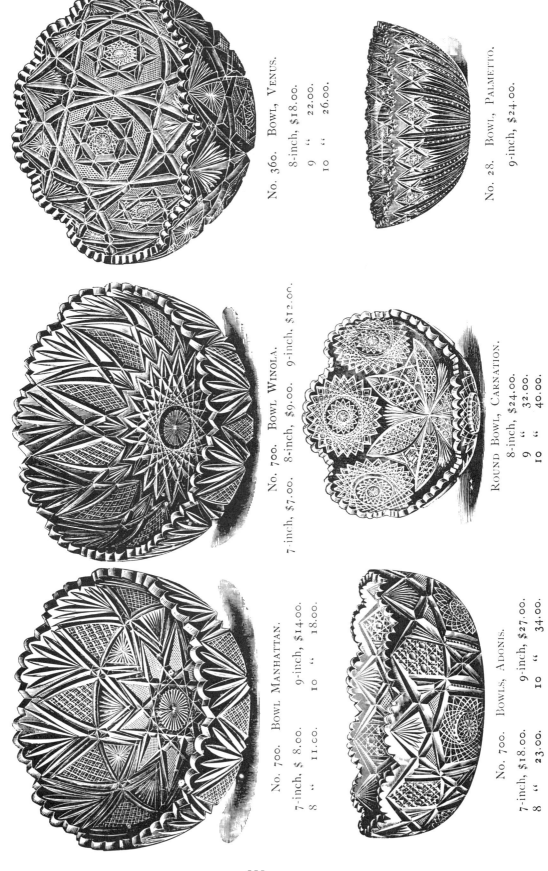

T. B. CLARK & COMPANY'S AMERICAN CUT GLASS.

No. 360. Bowl, Venus.
8-inch, $18.00.
9 " " 22.00.
10 " " 26.00.

No. 28. Bowl, Palmetto.
9-inch, $24.00.

No. 700. Bowl Winola.
7-inch, $7.00. 8-inch, $9.00. 9-inch, $12.00.

Round Bowl, Carnation.
8-inch, $24.00.
9 " " 32.00.
10 " " 40.00.

No. 700. Bowl Manhattan.
7-inch, $ 8.00. 9-inch, $14.00.
8 " " 11.00. 10 " " 18.00.

No. 700. Bowls, Adonis.
7-inch, $18.00. 9-inch, $27.00.
8 " " 23.00. 10 " " 34.00.

111

T. B. CLARK & COMPANY'S AMERICAN CUT GLASS.

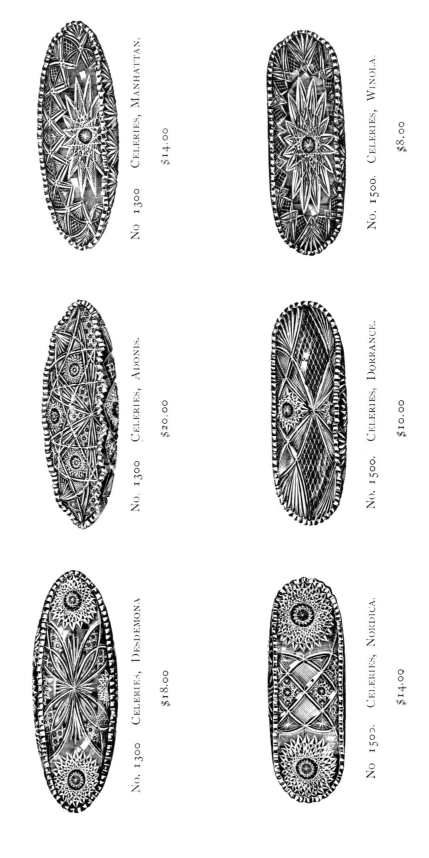

No. 1300   Celeries, Desdemona.
$18.00

No. 1300   Celeries, Adonis.
$20.00

No. 1300   Celeries, Manhattan.
$14.00

No. 1500.   Celeries, Nordica.
$14.00

No. 1500.   Celeries, Dorrance.
$10.00

No. 1500.   Celeries, Winola.
$8.00

T. B. CLARK & COMPANY'S AMERICAN CUT GLASS.

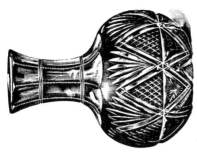

QT. C CARAFE, WINOLA.
$7.00.

QT. D CARAFE MANHATTAN.
$7.00.

QT. C CARAFE, HENRY VIII.
$9.00.

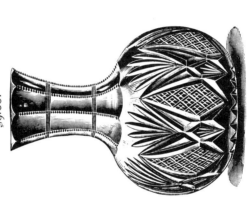

QT. D CARAFE WINOLA.
$6.00.

QT. C CARAFE, MANHATTAN.
$8.00.

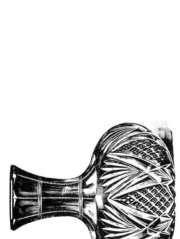

QT. C CARAFE, WINOLA.
$7.00.

QT. D CARAFE, JEWEL.
$7.00.

T. B. CLARK & COMPANY'S AMERICAN CUT GLASS.

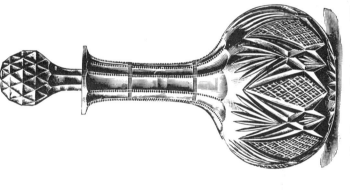

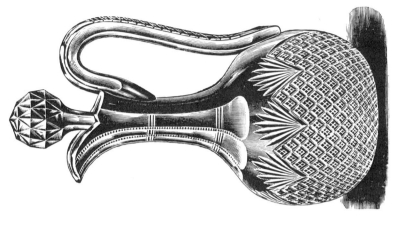

Quart Handled Decanter, Winola.
$12.00.

Quart No Handle Decanter, Winola.
$10.00.

Quart Handled Decanter, Straw and Fan.
$14.00.   Without Handle $12.00.

T. B. CLARK & COMPANY'S AMERICAN CUT GLASS.

No. 430. Decanter, Coral.
No Handle $25.00. Handled $30.00.

No. 750. Jug, Desdemona.
$36.00.

Qt. Globe Decanter, Manhattan.
No Handle $12.00. Handled $14.00.

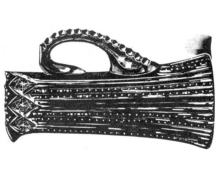

Flemish Jugs, Palmetto.
No. 2, $24.00. No. 1, $30.00.
No. 01, $36.00.

No. 880. Whiskey Flagon, Venus.
$18.00.

No. 40. Claret Jug, Arbutus.
With No. 202 A, Sterling Top.
$36.00.

T. B. CLARK & COMPANY'S AMERICAN CUT GLASS.

WIDE MOUTH JUG, JEWEL.

½ Pint $6.00.   Pint $8.00.   Qt. $10.50.
3 Pint. $14.00.   ½ Gallon $16.00.

WIDE MOUTH JUG, WINOLA.

½ Pint $6.00.   Pint $8.00.   Qt. $10.50.
3 Pint $14.00.   ½ Gallon $16.00.

WIDE MOUTH JUG, VENUS.

Pint $14.00.   Qt. $17.00.   3 Pint $20.00.

WIDE MOUTH JUG, ARBUTUS.

½ Pint $11.00.   Pint $13.00   Qt. $16.00.
3 Pint $19.00.   ½ Gallon $23.00.

No. 10. FLEMISH JUG, ADONIS.
$44.00.

PRISCILLA JUG, DESDEMONA.
$36.00.

T. B. CLARK & COMPANY'S AMERICAN CUT GLASS.

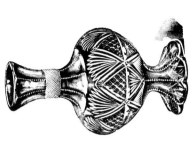

PRISCILLA CARAFE, MANHATTAN.
$18.00.

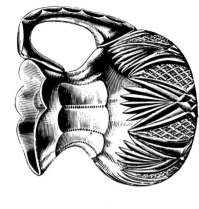

No. 82.   Qt. Jug, Winola.
$8.00.

No. 39.   Jug, Palmetto.
½ Gallon $27.00.

Quart Tankard Jug, Henry VIII.
$10.00.

Tankard Jug,   Palmetto.
Quart $20.00.   3 Pint 26.00.

WIDE MOUTH JUG, MANHATTAN.
½ Pint $6.00.   Pint $8.00.   Quart $10.50.
3 Pint $14.00.   ½ Gallon $16.00.

117

T. B. CLARK & COMPANY'S AMERICAN CUT GLASS.

ROUND NAPPY, JEWEL.

5-inch, Doz. $30.00.
6 " " 36.00.
7 " " 54.00.

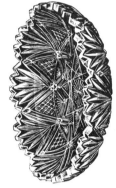

No. 200. NAPPY, MANHATTAN.

7-inch, Each $7.50.
8 " " 9.00.
9 " " 11.50.
10 " " 14.00.

ROUND NAPPY, WINOLA.

5-inch, Doz. $30.00.
6 " " 36.00.
7 " " 54.00.

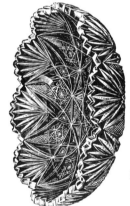

No. 200. NAPPY, ARBUTUS.

7-inch, Each $10.00.
8 " " 12.00.
9 " " 15.00.
10 " " 18.00.

ROUND NAPPY, MANHATTAN.

5-inch, Doz. $34.00.
6 " " 42.00.
7 " " 60.00.

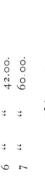

No. 200. NAPPY, DESDEMONA.

7-inch, Each $12.00.
8 " " 15.00.
9 " " 17.00.
10 " " 19.00.

T. B. CLARK & COMPANY'S AMERICAN CUT GLASS.

No. 1313.   Bon Bon, Manhattan.
$4.50.

No. 1075.   Bon Bon, Venus.
$7.00.

No. 1111.   Bon Bon, Arbutus.
$5.50.

No. 131.   Bon Bon, Jewel.
$3.00.

No 514.   Bon Bon, Adonis.
$10.00.

No. 1717.   Bon Bon, Manhattan.
$4.50.

T. B. CLARK & COMPANY'S AMERICAN CUT GLASS.

No. 4 S.   Bon Bon, St. George.
$4.00.

No. 360.   Nappy, Venus.
8-inch, $17.00.
9   "   19.00.

No. 30.   Footed Bowl, Manhattan.
6-inch, $8.00.

No. 205.   Nappy, Adonis.
9-inch, $21.00.

No. 12 S.   Bon Bon, Dorrance.
$6.00.

No. 300.   Nappy, Desdemona.
$18.00.

T. B. CLARK & COMPANY'S AMERICAN CUT GLASS.

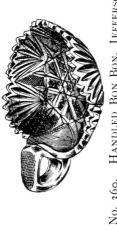

No. 13 S.   Bon Bon, Winola.
$4.00.

No. 6 S.   Bon Bon, St. George.
$4.00.

No. 360.   Handled Bon Bon, Jefferson.

5-inch, $4.00.
6   "   5.00.

No. 360.   Handled Bon Bon, Irving.

5-inch, $4.00.
6   "   5.00.

Rd. Handled Bon Bon, St. George.

5-inch, $3.50.
6   "   4.00.

No. 200.   Nappy, Jewel.

7-inch, $7.50.
8   "   9.00.
9   "   11.50.
10   "   14.00.

T. B. CLARK & COMPANY'S AMERICAN CUT GLASS.

7-inch Round Plate, Venus.
$84.00 per Doz.

3 Lip Oil Huron.
$30.00 per Doz.

No. 1818.   Bon Bon, Jewel.
$4.00.

No. 1040.   Oil, Manhattan.
$56.00 per Doz.

No. 1010.   Bon Bon, Jewel.
$4.50.

Nest Table Salt, Venus.
$6.00 Each.

T. B. CLARK & COMPANY'S AMERICAN CUT GLASS.

No. 7. Tea Caddy, Henry VIII.
With Sterling Top, No. 37 A. $11.00.

Syrup Jug, Henry VIII.
No. 5. Sm. Size, $7.00.
No. 14. Lg. Size, $8.00.
Plated Top.

No. 10. Sugar Sifter, Henry VIII.
With Sterling Top, No. 45 A. $12.00.

No. 2223. Pepper or Salt, Henry VIII.
Sterling Top, $5.00 Each.

Tobasco Sauce Bottle, Henry VIII.
Sterling Top, $5.00.

Pepper Sauce Bottle, Jewel.
Sterling Top, $7.00.

Bells, Jewel.
Large Size, $3.50.
Small Size, $3.00.

Worcestershire Sauce
Bottle, Jewel. $7.00.

123

T. B. CLARK & COMPANY'S AMERICAN CUT GLASS.

EMPRESS SPOON HOLDER,
JEWEL. $6.50.

No. 545. CREAM SET, WINOLA.

No. 1. Large Size, $11.00. No. 2. Small Size, $8.00.

No. 640. SPOON TRAY, MANHATTAN.
$7.00.

No. 645. CREAM SET, ARBUTUS.
$15.00.

No. 745. CREAM SET, VENUS.
$17.00.

T. B. CLARK & COMPANY'S AMERICAN CUT GLASS.

No. 520. CLARETS, WINOLA.
$20.50 per Doz.

No. 520. WINES, WINOLA.
$18.50 per Doz.

No. 520. SAUCER CHAMPAGNE,
WINOLA, $25.00 per Doz.

No. 520. SHERRY, WINOLA.
$18.50 per Doz.

No. 520. GOBLET, WINOLA.
$25.00 per Doz.

No. 520. CORDIALS, WINOLA.
$18.00 per Doz.

125

T. B. CLARK & COMPANY'S AMERICAN CUT GLASS.

No. 520. ½ Pint Tumbler. Arbutus. $36.00 per Doz.

No. 750. Tumbler, Winola. $11.00 per Doz.

No. 520. ½ Pint Tumbler, Manhattan. $24.00 per Doz.

No. 895. ½ Pint Tumbler, Henry VIII. $24.00 per Doz.

No. 520. Whiskey Tumbler, Winola. $18.00 per Doz.

No. 520. ½ Pint Tumbler, Coral. $42.00 per Doz.

No. 520. Champagne Tumbler Winola. $18.00 per Doz

No. 520. ½ Pint Tumbler, Jewel. $24.00 per Doz.

T. B. CLARK & COMPANY'S AMERICAN CUT GLASS.

No. 1073. PUNCH CUP & PLATE,
JEWEL. { Plates, Doz. $24 00.
{ Cups, " 24.00.

No. 520. H. E. FINGER BOWLS, WINOLA.
$48.00 per Doz.

No. 520. P. E. FINGER BOWLS,
JEWEL. $25.60 per Doz.

No. 520. P. E. FINGER BOWLS, WINOLA.
$25.60 per Doz.

No. 240. HANDLED LEMONADES,
JEWEL. $24 00 per Doz.

No. 287. TUMBLERS.
No. 10 Cutting, $6.00 per Doz.

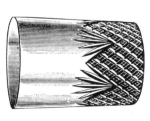

No. 520. HANDLED LEMONADES, WINOLA.
$20.00 per Doz.

127

T. B. CLARK & COMPANY'S AMERICAN CUT GLASS.

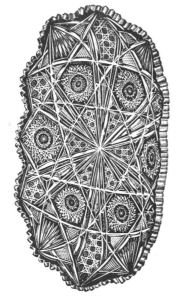

No. 1616.   ICE CREAM TRAY, ADONIS.
$40.00.

No. 1616.   ICE CREAM TRAY, WINOLA.
$23.00.

No. 1616.   ICE CREAM TRAY, VENUS.
$30.00

No. 1616.   ICE CREAM TRAY, MANHATTAN.
$25.00.

128

T. B. CLARK & COMPANY'S AMERICAN CUT GLASS.

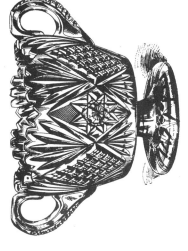

No. 1360.   Ice Tub, Jewel.
$15.00.

Bulb Vase, Heroic.

No. 1. Lg. Size, $14.00.   No. 2. Sm. Size, $10.00.

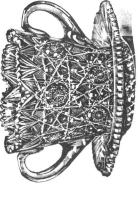

Ice Tub & Plate, Coral.
$32.00.

No. 1192.   Vases, Jewel.

7-inch, $3.00.   8-inch, $4.00.
10   "   5.00.   12   "   7.00.

Butter Tub & Plate, Manhattan.
$15.00.

Cheese Cover & Plate, Manhattan.
6-inch, $22.00.

T. B. CLARK & COMPANY'S AMERICAN CUT GLASS.

PINK VASE, WINOLA. $3.50.

NO. 1194.   VASE, HENRY VIII.
7-inch, $4.00 Each.   8-inch, $5.00 Each.
10 "   12 "   10.00 "
15-inch, $15.00 Each.

NO. 26.   VASE, HENRY VIII.
4-inch, $9.00.   6-inch, $15.00.

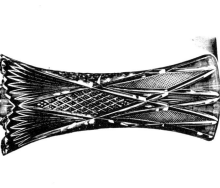

NO. 25.   VASES, HENRY VIII.
7-inch, $6.50.   9-inch, $9.00.   12-inch, $14.00.

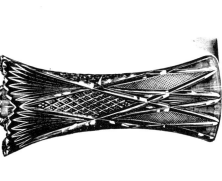

ROSE GLOBE, MANHATTAN.
6-inch, $12.00.   7-inch, $14.00.   8-inch, $16.00.

BULB VASE, PALMETTO.
No. 1.   Large Size, $15.00.
No. 2.   Small Size,   12.00.

T. B. CLARK & COMPANY'S AMERICAN CUT GLASS.

PRISCILLA VASE, DESDEMONA.
$33.00.

No. 1082. VASE, PALMETTO.

7-inch, $ 9.00.
8   "   " 11.00.
10 "   " 18.00.
12 "   " 21.00.
15 "   " 30.00.
18 "   " 36.00.

No. 1082. VASE, ADONIS.

15-inch, $34.00.
18 "   " 40.00.

No. 25. VASE, ORIENT.

9-inch, $16.00 Each.
12 "   " 24.00 "

T. B. CLARK & COMPANY'S AMERICAN CUT GLASS.

GLOBE COLOGNE, JEWEL.

No. 1. (24 oz.) $11.00 Each.
" 2. (18 ") 9.00 "
" 3. (9 ") 6.50 "
" 4. (6 ") 5.00 "

GLOBE COLOGNE, VENUS.

No. 1. $16.00 Each. No. 3. $10.00 Each.
" 2. 12.00 " " 4. 9.00 "

PUNCH LADLE, DESDEMONA.
$14.00.

ROUND COLOGNE, JEWEL.
6 oz. $5.25 Each. 8 oz. $6.00 Each.
12 oz. $7.50 Each.

SALAD FORK & SPOON, MANHATTAN.
Pair, $14.00.

No. 30. SQUARE COLOGNE, ST. GEORGE.
8 oz. $8.50 Each. 12 oz. $10.00 Each.

UNITED STATES GLASS COMPANY

Eighteen of the most important western Pennsylvania, eastern Ohio and West Virginia glass manufacturers were merged on July 1, 1891, to form the United States Glass Company. Similar moves to consolidate operations were being made at the time in other American industries. This merger was not, however, one of the happier business marriages of convenience, not at least in the opinion of the skilled glass workers, firmly organized in the American Flint Glass Workers' Union. Of the original 18 companies, only six survived in 1904 following the great strike of 1893–96, which the company fought to gain control over the workers' output, and succeeding economic difficulties.

The 18 original companies and the factory letters assigned to them are as follows: Adams & Company, Pittsburgh (A); Bryce Brothers, Pittsburgh (B); Challinor, Taylor & Company, Tarentum (C); George Duncan & Sons, Pittsburgh (D); Richards & Hartley, Tarentum (E); Ripley & Company, Pittsburgh (F); Gillinder & Sons, Greensburg (G); Hobbs Glass Company, Wheeling, West Virginia (H); Columbia Glass Company, Findlay, Ohio (J); O'Hara Glass Company, Pittsburgh (L); King Glass Company, Pittsburgh (K); Bellaire Goblet Company, Findlay, Ohio (M); Nickel Plate Glass Company, Fostoria, Ohio (N); Central Glass Company, Wheeling, West Virginia (O); Doyle & Company, Pittsburgh (P); A. J. Beatty & Sons, Tiffin, Ohio (R); A. J. Beatty & Sons, Steubenville, Ohio (S); and Novelty Glass Company, Fostoria, Ohio (T).

In 1904, the year the succeeding catalog pages appeared, only Adams, Bryce, Doyle, Ripley, King and A. J. Beatty of Tiffin were in production.

The following pages reproduce only the named sets of pressed ware, with the exception of # 15055 (Minnesota), # 15068 (Connecticut) and # 15083 (Carolina). For the most part, the main pieces of the set are shown and not such extra pieces as vases, salad bowls and cracker jars. The remainder of this 158-page catalog is devoted to goblets, beer mugs, candlesticks, various types of jars, tumblers, jugs and lamps.

UNITED STATES GLASS CO. PITTSBURG PA. U. S. A.

Made in Crystal, also Magenta, Gold and Tulip Decorations.

15082 or Columbia Pattern

Tumbler, Ground.

Drinking Mug, also make Flared

Large Tankard, also make small and medium sizes.

½ Gallon Pitcher, also make ¼ Gallon and ¾ gallon sizes.

Handled Horse Radish and Cover.

Large S. or P., S.P.T., also make medium and small sizes.

Ordinary Salt and Pepper, N.T., also make with Dome, N. T. Brit. N. T.

Finger Bowl.

Goblet.

Hotel Sugar and Cover.

Toothpick.

Egg Cup.

Wine Flared, also make straight shape.

Match Safe.

Sundae Cup and Plate.

Handled Jelly

Butter and Cover.

Medium Sugar, Open.

Custard.

Lemonade.

5 inch Footed Sweetmeat.

Spoon.

Medium Cream.

Cream.

4 inch Deep Nappy.

5 inch Saucer Nappy.

Large Molasses Can Britannia Top, also made with S. P. T. & N. Top.

8½ inch Deep Nappy, also make 4½, 5½, 6½ and 7½ inch sizes.

11½ inch Saucer Nappy, also make 4½, 6, 7, 8½ and 10 inch sizes.

Small Molasses Can, S. P. T.

Sugar and Cover.

Oil Bottle, Ground Stopper.

134

UNITED STATES GLASS CO., PITTSBURG, PA., U. S. A.

15077 or Michigan Pattern.

Made in Plain Crystal, also Sunrise and Gold Decorations.

6 ounce Tankard Cream.

Tumbler.

½ Gallon Tankard, also make for Silver Rim.

Small Butter and Cover.

Gainsboro Hdld. Nappy.

Custard.

3 Pint Jug.

5½ inch Round Plate.

Sherbet, Handled.

Butter and Cover.

Pickle Dish.

Small Salt or Pepper, S.P.T.

Goblet.

Shaker, Salt or Pepper, D.N.T.

Spoon.

Hotel Salt or Pepper, S.P.T.

Water Bottle.

Olive Dish.

Finger Bowl.

Cream.

Oil or Vinegar.

Sugar and Cover.

4½ inch Nappy.

8½ inch Nappy, also make 4, 6 and 7 inch sizes.

5 inch Berry Nappy.

10 inch Berry Nappy, also make 7½, 8½ and 4 inch sizes.

135

UNITED STATES GLASS CO., PITTSBURG, PA., U. S. A.

15078 or Manhattan Pattern.

9½ inch Fruit Bowl, Footed, also make 10½ inch Flared Fruit Bowl.

7½ inch Preserve Dish.

½ Gallon Tankard, also make for Silver Rim.

Tumbler.

Ice Tea Tumbler.

5 inch Plate.

6 inch Flat Jelly.

8 inch Celery Tray.

½ Gallon Pitcher.

Tall Celery.

Oval Individual Cream.

5 inch Trinket Tray.

Water Bottle.

Butter and Cover.

Oval Individual Sugar, Open, with and without Inside Ledge.

4½ inch Gainsboro Handled Nappy.

5 inch Saucer Nappy.

Spoon Holder.

4½ inch Nappy.

4½ inch Deep Nappy, also made with Inside Ledge.

4½ inch Fruit Nappy.

12½ inch Saucer Nappy, also make 9 and 10 inch sizes and 9½, 11 and 12½ inch plates.

Cream Pitcher.

Sugar and Cover.

9½ inch Nappy, also make 7 and 8½ inch sizes.

11 inch Berry Nappy, also make 8 and 9½ inch sizes.

9½ inch Fruit Nappy.

136

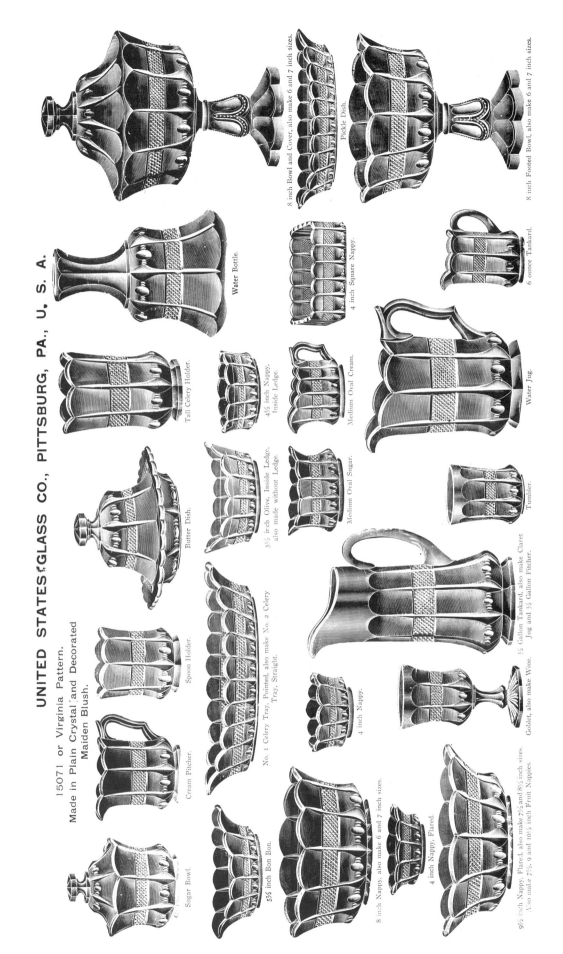

UNITED STATES GLASS CO., PITTSBURG, PA., U. S. A.

15071 or Virginia Pattern.
Made in Plain Crystal and Decorated Maiden Blush.

8 inch Bowl and Cover, also make 6 and 7 inch sizes.

Pickle Dish.

8 inch Footed Bowl, also make 6 and 7 inch sizes.

Water Bottle.

4 inch Square Nappy.

6 ounce Tankard.

Tall Celery Holder.

4½ inch Nappy, Inside Ledge.

Medium Oval Cream.

Water Jug.

Butter Dish.

5½ inch Olive, Inside Ledge, also made without Ledge.

Medium Oval Sugar.

Tumbler.

Spoon Holder.

No. 1 Celery Tray, Pointed, also make No. 2 Celery Tray, Straight.

½ Gallon Tankard, also make Claret Jug and ½ Gallon Pitcher.

Cream Pitcher.

4 inch Nappy.

Goblet, also make Wine.

Sugar Bowl.

5½ inch Bon Bon.

8 inch Nappy, also make 6 and 7 inch sizes.

4 inch Nappy, Flared.

9½ inch Nappy, Flared, also make 7½ and 8½ inch sizes. Also make 7½, 9 and 10½ inch Fruit Nappies.

137

UNITED STATES GLASS CO., PITTSBURG, PA. U. S. A.

15073 or State of Oregon Pattern.

English Butter Dish.

Oil or Vinegar Bottle.

Tumbler.

8 inch Bowl and Cover, also make 6 and 7 inch sizes and 6, 7 and 8 inch Open Bowls.

Spoon Holder, Flat.

10 inch Salver, also make 8 and 9 inch sizes.

5 inch Footed Jelly and Cover, also make without Cover.

Cream Pitcher Flat.

Handled Mug, also make with Notched Cover called Horse Radish.

Celery Holder.

Sugar Bowl, Flat.

Molasses Can, Tin Top.

Butted Dish, Flanged, also make Butter Dish, Flat.

Salt or Pepper.

Toothpick Holder.

Goblet, also make Wine.

Bread Plate.

Spoon Holder, Footed.

3½ inch Comport.

Cream Pitcher, Footed.

4 inch Nappy, also make 3½ inch size.

Pickle Dish, also make Olive Dish, same shape.

½ Gallon Pitcher, also make Pint and Quart sizes.

Sugar Bowl, Footed.

8 inch Nappy, also make 3½, 4, 6 and 7 inch sizes.

9½ inch Oval Dish, also make 7½, 10½ and 12½ inch sizes.

10 inch Footed Fruit Bowl, also make 7¼ and 8½ inch sizes.

138

UNITED STATES GLASS CO., PITTSBURG PA. U. S. A.

15047 or Colonial Pattern.

Cracker Jar and Cover.

Wine Glass, also make Goblet.

Tumbler.

6 inch Bowl and Cover, also make 7 and 8 inch.

Celery Holder.

Hotel Vinegar.

Individual Salt.

Cream Pitcher, also make Footed Spoon.

8 inch Oval Dish.

6 inch Bowl, also make 7 and 8 inch.

½ Gal. Pitcher. This illustration ¼ size.

Footed Sugar Bowl.

Individual Sugar, also make without Handles, called Toothpick.

Water Bottle.

Butter Dish.

Olive Dish.

Hotel Salt or Pepper, S.P.T.

Syrup Jug, Ewer Top.

Shaker, Salt or Pepper, S.P.T.

Hotel Spoon.

Pickle Dish.

Low Foot Jelly.

Molasses Can, Glass Top.

Hotel Cream, also make Individual Cream, same shape.

8 inch, Nappy, also make 4, 4½, 5, 6 and 7 inch sizes.

10 inch Crimped Fruit Bowl, also make 7, 8 and 9 inch sizes and 7½, 8½ and 9½ inch Comports, Flared.

Oil or Vinegar, make Decanter same shape.

Hotel Sugar Bowl.

6 in. Comport and Cover, also make 7 and 8 in. and 6, 7 and 8 in, no Cover, and 8 in. with Notched Cover.

139

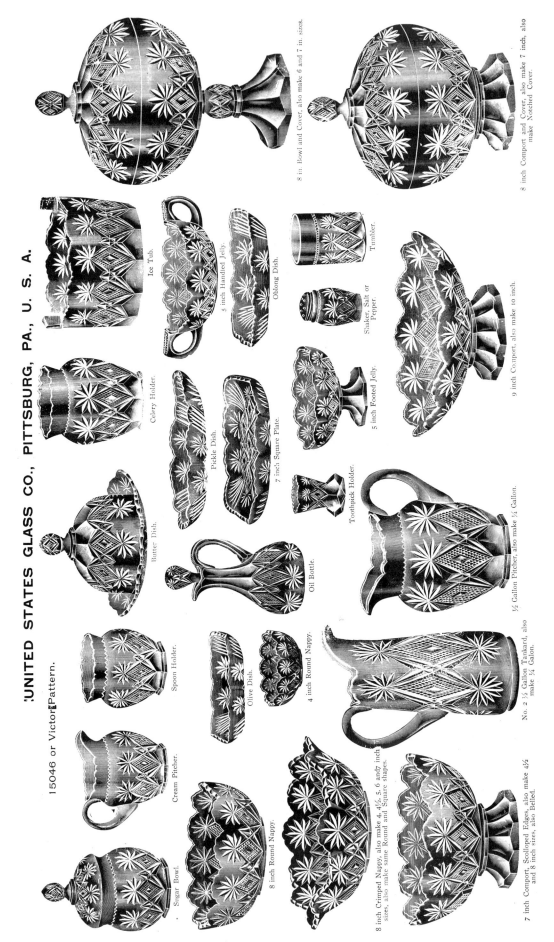

UNITED STATES GLASS CO., PITTSBURG, PA., U. S. A.

15046 or Victor Pattern.

8 in Bowl and Cover, also make 6 and 7 in. sizes.

8 inch Comport and Cover, also make 7 inch, also make Notched Cover.

Ice Tub.

5 inch Handled Jelly.

Oblong Dish.

Tumbler.

Shaker, Salt or Pepper.

Celery Holder.

Pickle Dish.

7 inch Square Plate.

5 inch Footed Jelly.

9 inch Comport, also make 10 inch.

Butter Dish.

Toothpick Holder.

Oil Bottle.

½ Gallon Pitcher, also make ¼ Gallon.

Spoon Holder.

Olive Dish.

4 inch Round Nappy.

No. 2 ½ Gallon Tankard, also make ¼ Galon.

Cream Pitcher.

8 inch Round Nappy.

8 inch Crimped Nappy, also make 4, 4½, 5, 6 and 7 inch sizes, also make same Round and Square shapes.

Sugar Bowl.

7 inch Comport. Scolloped Edges, also make 4½ and 8 inch sizes, also Belled.

140

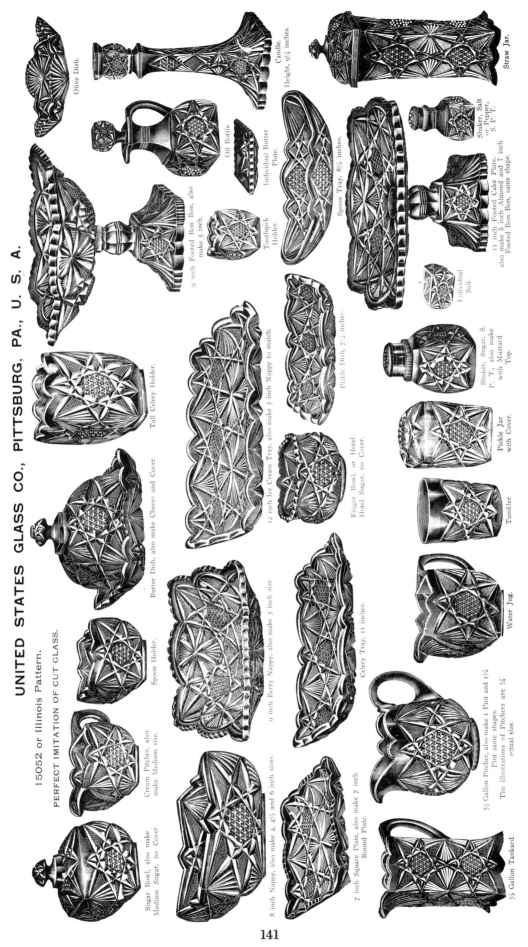

UNITED STATES GLASS CO., PITTSBURG, PA., U. S. A.

15052 or Illinois Pattern.

PERFECT IMITATION OF CUT GLASS.

Olive Dish.

Candle.
Height, 9¼ inches.

Straw Jar.

Oil Bottle.

Individual Butter
Plate.

9 inch Footed Bon Bon, also
make 5 inch.

Toothpick
Holder.

Spoon Tray, 8½ inches.

Shaker, Salt
or Pepper,
S. P. T.

11 inch Footed Cake Plate.
also make 5 inch Almond and 7 inch
Footed Bon Bon, same shape.

Individual
Salt.

Cream Pitcher, also
make Medium size.

Tall Celery Holder.

Butter Dish, also make Cheese and Cover.

12 inch Ice Cream Tray, also make 5 inch Nappy to match.

Pickle Dish, 7½ inches.

Shaker, Sugar, S.
P. T., also make
with Mustard
Top.

Spoon Holder.

9 inch Berry Nappy, also make 5 inch size

Finger Bowl, or Hotel
Hotel Sugar, no Cover.

Pickle Jar
with Cover.

Sugar Bowl, also make
Medium Sugar, no Cover.

8 inch Nappy, also make 4, 4½ and 6 inch sizes.

Celery Tray, 11 inches.

Tumbler.

Water Jug.

7 inch Square Plate, also make 7 inch
Round Plate.

½ Gallon Pitcher, also make 1 Pint and 1½
Pint same shapes.
The illustrations of Pitchers are ¼
actual size.

½ Gallon Tankard.

141

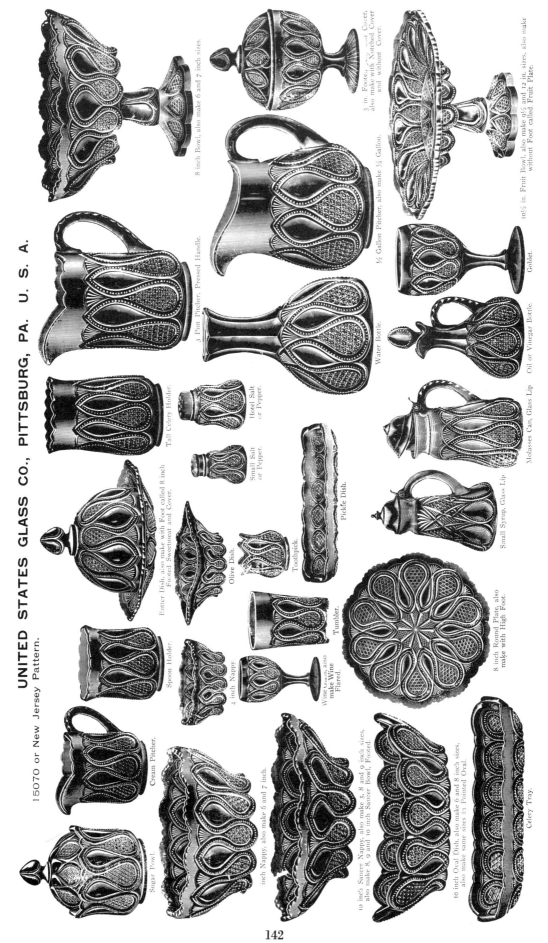

UNITED STATES GLASS CO., PITTSBURG, PA. U. S. A.

15070 or New Jersey Pattern.

8 inch Bowl, also make 6 and 7 inch sizes.

5 in. Footed ...... and Cover,
also make with Notched Cover
and without Cover.

10½ in. Fruit Bowl, also make 9½ and 12 in. sizes, also make
without Foot called Fruit Plate.

3 Pint Pitcher, Pressed Handle.

½ Gallon Pitcher, also make ¼ Gallon.

Goblet.

Water Bottle.

Oil or Vinegar Bottle.

Tall Celery Holder.

Hotel Salt
or Pepper.

Molasses Can, Glass Lip

Small Salt
or Pepper.

Pickle Dish.

Butter Dish, also make with Foot called 8 inch
Footed Sweetmeat and Cover.

Olive Dish.

Toothpick.

Small Syrup, Glass Lip

Tumbler.

8 inch Round Plate, also
make with High Foot.

Spoon Holder.

4 inch Nappy.

Wine Glass, also
make Wine
Flared.

Cream Pitcher.

inch Nappy, also make 6 and 7 inch.

10 inch Saucer Nappy, also make 5, 8 and 9 inch sizes,
also make 8, 9 and 10 inch Saucer Bowl, Footed.

10 inch Oval Dish, also make 6 and 8 inch sizes,
also make same sizes in Pointed Oval.

Sugar Bowl.

Celery Tray.

142

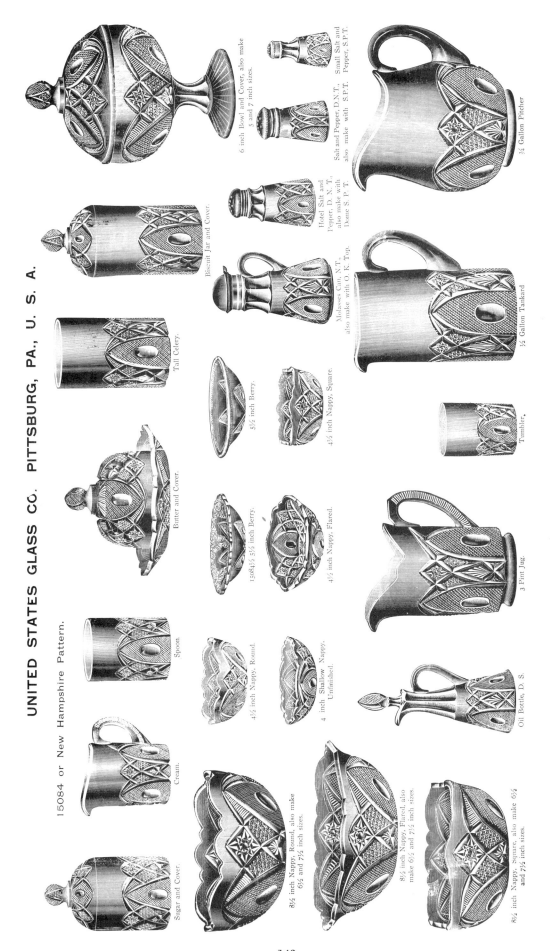

UNITED STATES GLASS CO. PITTSBURG, PA., U. S. A.

15084 or New Hampshire Pattern.

6 inch Bowl and Cover, also make 5 and 7 inch sizes.

Small Salt and Pepper, S.P.T.

Salt and Pepper, D.N.T., also make with S. P. T.

¾ Gallon Pitcher

Hotel Salt and Pepper, D. N. T., also make with Dome S. P. T.

Biscuit Jar and Cover.

Molasses Can, N. T., also make with O. K. Top.

½ Gallon Tankard

Tall Celery.

5½ inch Berry.

4½ inch Nappy, Square.

Tumbler.

Butter and Cover.

150 4½ 5½ inch Berry.

4½ inch Nappy, Flared.

3 Pint Jug.

Spoon.

4½ inch Nappy, Round.

4 inch Shallow Nappy, Unfinished.

Oil Bottle, D. S.

Cream.

8½ inch Nappy, Round, also make 6½ and 7½ inch sizes.

8½ inch Nappy, Flared, also make 6½ and 7½ inch sizes.

Sugar and Cover.

8½ inch Nappy, Square, also make 6½ and 7½ inch sizes.

UNITED STATED GLASS CO., PITTSBURG, PA., U. S. A.

15075 or Nevada Pattern.

8 inch Bowl and Cover, also make 6 and 7 inch sizes.

8 inch Bowl, Open, also make 6 and 7 inch sizes.

Pickle or 6 inch Oval.

Shaker, Salt or Pepper.

Hotel Salt or Pepper, Dome, Nickle Top.

Finger Bowl.

Cracker Jar and Cover.

Tall Celery.

10 inch Salver.

Custard, also make Sherbe, no Handle.

Tumbler.

Butter and Cover.

4½ inch Gainsboro Handled Nappy.

½ Gallon Tankard, also make 3 Pint Pitcher.

Spoon.

Toothpick.

11 inch Oval Dish, also make 7, 8, 9 and 10 inch sizes.

Table Salt.

Cream.

Individual Salt.

Water Jug.

Sugar and Cover.

4½ inch Nappy, also make 4 and 5 inch and 4½ inch Flat Nappy.

8 inch Nappy, also make 6 and 7 inch and 4½, 6, 7 and 8 inch with Covers.

Oil or Vinegar, D. S.

Molasses Can, T. T.

144

UNITED STATES GLASS CO.; PITTSBURG, PA., U. S. A.

15067 or Texas Pattern.

8 inch Footed Berry.

Individual Cream.

10 inch Low Salver, also make 9 and 10 inch High Foot.

6 in. Footed Bowl and Cover. make 7 and 8 in. sizes.

Toothpick Holder.

Individual Sugar, also make with Notched Cover called Horseradish.

Shaker, Salt or Pepper, also make Hotel size.

Pickle Dish, also make Celery Tray same shape.

9 inch Plate.

8 inch Preserve Dish.

Tall Celery Holder.

Olive Dish.

Oil or Vinegar Bottle.

4 inch Berry.

5 inch Footed Jelly Bowl.

Wine Glass.

Goblet.

4 inch Nappy.

6 inch Berry and Cover, also make 7 and 8 inch sizes.

Molasses Can, O. K. Top, also make with Nickle Top.

4 inch Low Foot Jelly, also make 5 inch Flared.

3 Pint Pitcher, Pressed Handle. Illustration ¼ actual size.

Tumbler.

9½ inch Berry, also make 4½, 7½ and 8½ inch sizes, also make 7½, 8½ and 9½ inch Footed.

8 inch Nappy.

8½ inch Saucer Nappy, also make 7½ and 9½ inch sizes.

7 inch Scolloped Nappy, also make 6 and 8 inch sizes.

145

UNITED STATES GLASS CO. PITTSBURG PA. U S A.

15059 or California Pattern.

7 inch Bowl and Cover, also make 8 and 9 inch sizes.

7 inch Nappy and Cover, also make 8 and 9 inch sizes.

9 inch Salver.

Footed Jelly and Cover.

Footed Jelly Bowl

Australian Sugar and Cover, Low Foot.

Olive Dish.

Footed Cake Plate.

7 inch Bowl, also make 8 and 9 inch sizes.

Tall Celery Holder.

Toothpick Holder.

Goblet.

Tumbler.

Butter Dish.

Pickle Dish.

Oil or Vinegar Bottle.

Water Jug, Illustrations of Pitchers are ¼ actual size.

Spoon Holder.

3½ inch Nappy.

Wine Glass.

Shaker, Salt or Pepper.

½ Gallon Tankard. Illustrations of Pitchers are ¼ actual size.

Cream Pitcher.

Sugar Bowl.

9 inch Nappy, also make 4, 4½, 6, 7 and 8 inch sizes.

Bread Tray.

Preserve Dish.

Square Plate.

Celery Tray.

146

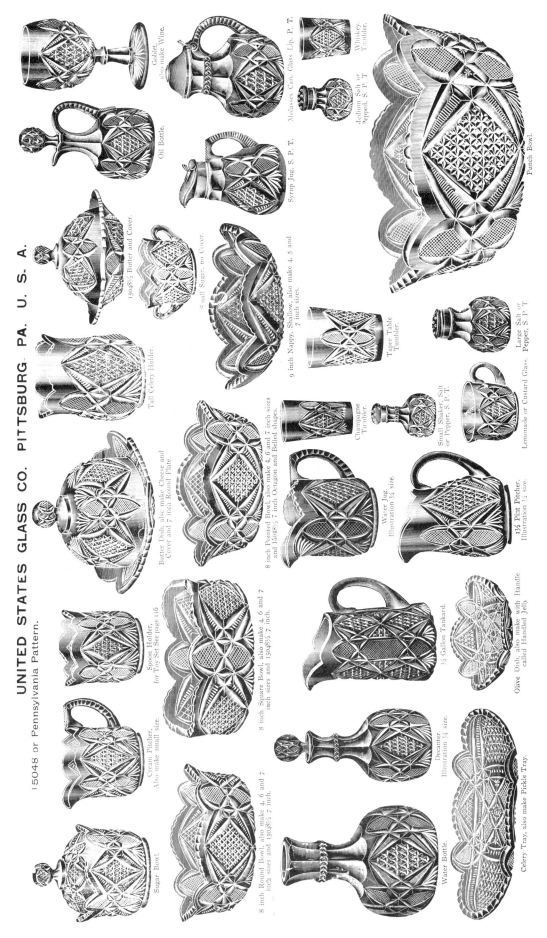

UNITED STATES GLASS CO. PITTSBURG. PA. U. S. A.

15048 or Pennsylvania Pattern.

Goblet, also make Wine.

Oil Bottle.

Whiskey Tumbler.

Molasses Can. Glass Lip. P. T.

Medium Salt or Pepper. S. P. T.

Punch Bowl.

Syrup Jug, S. P. T.

15048½ Butter and Cover.

Small Sugar. no Cover.

Tall Celery Holder.

9 inch Nappy. Shallow, also make 4, 5 and 7 inch sizes.

Taper Table Tumbler.

Large Salt or Pepper, S. P. T.

Butter Dish, also make Cheese and Cover and 7 inch Round Plate.

8 inch Pointed Bowl, also make 4, 6 and 7 inch sizes and 15048½ 7 inch Octagon and Belled shapes.

Champagne Tumbler.

Small Shaker, Salt or Pepper, S. P. T.

Lemonade or Custard Glass.

Water Jug. Illustration ¼ size.

1¼ Pint Pitcher. Illustration ¼ size.

Spoon Holder, for Toy Set See page 116

8 inch Square Bowl, also make 4, 6 and 7 inch sizes and 15048½ 7 inch.

½ Gallon Tankard.

Olive Dish, also make with Handle called Handled Jelly.

Cream Pitcher, Also make small size.

8 inch Round Bowl, also make 4, 6 and 7 inch sizes and 15048½ 7 inch.

Decanter. Illustration ¼ size.

Sugar Bowl.

Water Bottle.

Celery Tray, also make Pickle Tray.

147

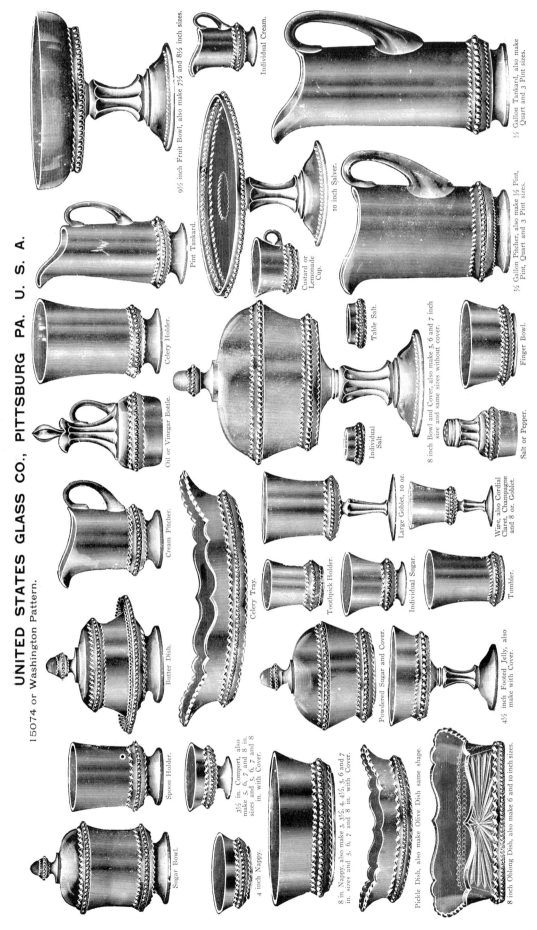

UNITED STATES GLASS CO., PITTSBURG PA. U. S. A.

15074 or Washington Pattern.

9½ inch Fruit Bowl, also make 7½ and 8½ inch sizes.

Individual Cream.

½ Gallon Tankard, also make Quart and 3 Pint sizes.

Pint Tankard.

10 inch Salver.

½ Gallon Pitcher, also make ½ Pint, Pint, Quart and 3 Pint sizes.

Celery Holder.

Custard or Lemonade Cup.

Table Salt.

Finger Bowl.

Oil or Vinegar Bottle.

Individual Salt

8 inch Bowl and Cover, also make 5, 6 and 7 inch size and same sizes without cover.

Salt or Pepper.

Cream Pitcher.

Celery Tray.

Large Goblet, 10 oz.

Wine, also Cordial Claret, Champagne and 8 oz. Goblet.

Butter Dish.

Toothpick Holder.

Individual Sugar.

Tumbler.

Powdered Sugar and Cover.

4½ inch Footed Jelly, also make with Cover.

Spoon Holder.

3½ in. Comport, also make 5, 6, 7 and 8 in. sizes and 5, 6, 7 and 8 in. with Cover.

Sugar Bowl.

4 inch Nappy.

8 in. Nappy, also make 3, 3½, 4, 4½, 5, 6 and 7 in. sizes and 5, 6, 7 and 8 in. with Cover.

Pickle Dish, also make Olive Dish same shape.

8 inch Oblong Dish, also make 6 and 10 inch sizes.

148

UNITED STATED GLASS CO., PITTSBURG, PA., U. S. A.

15057 or Colorado Pattern.

5 inch G. W. Comport, also make 4 and 6 inch sizes.

8 inch Comport, Crimped, also make 4, 5, 6 and 7 inch sizes.

7 inch Banana Dish.

5 inch G. W. Comport, Handled also make 4 inch.

Cafe Handled, also make without Handles.

Cheese Plate.

Butter Dish.

7 inch Comport, Round, also make 4, 5, 7 and 8 inch sizes.

Violet Bowl.

Small Sherbet, also make Large.

Toothpick Holder.

Spoon Holder.

7 inch Comport, Flared, also make 4, 5, 6 and 8 inch sizes.

6 inch Bowl. Crimped, also make 5, 7 and 8 inch sizes and 5, 6, 7 and 8 inch Flared.

Cream Pitcher.

Individual Cream.

Small Custard.

Sugar Bowl.

Individual Sugar, also make with two Handles.

Large Custard.

Tumbler, also make Handled.

149

UNITED STATES GLASS CO., PITTSBURG, PA., U. S. A.

15079 or Wisconsin Pattern.

7 inch Bowl and Cover, also make 6 and 8 inch sizes.

Condiment Set viz: Tall Salt and Pepper, Mustard and Horse Radish, also make with Salt and Pepper, Ind. Sugar and Cream.

9½ inch Saucer Bowl, also make 8½ and 10½ inch sizes.

Handled Butter and Cover, also make with Notched Cover.

Molasses Can, Tin Top, also make with Pat. Tin Top and Nickel Top.

Cup, also make with Saucer.

Hotel Sugar and Cover, also make without Cover.

Drinking Mug.

5 inch Footed Sweetmeat and Cover, also make with Notched Cover and without Cover.

Toothpick.

6 inch Handled Oval and Cover.

Small Butter and Cover, also make with Notched Cover.

Oil Bottle, D. S., also make without Handle.

Wine.

Tall Celery.

Tall Shaker, Salt or Pepper.

5 inch Saucer.

Butter and Cover.

Individual Sugar and Cover.

Individual Cream.

Shaker, Salt or Pepper.

Sugar Sifter.

Tumbler.

Spoon.

4 inch Nappy.

5½ inch Handled Nappy.

¼ Gallon Pitcher, also make 3 Pint Pitcher.

Cream.

8 inch Nappy, also make 6 and 7 inch sizes.

Pickle Dish.

8 inch Preserve, also make 6 inch.

6 inch Handled Oval, Open.

Celery Tray.

Sugar and Cover.

150

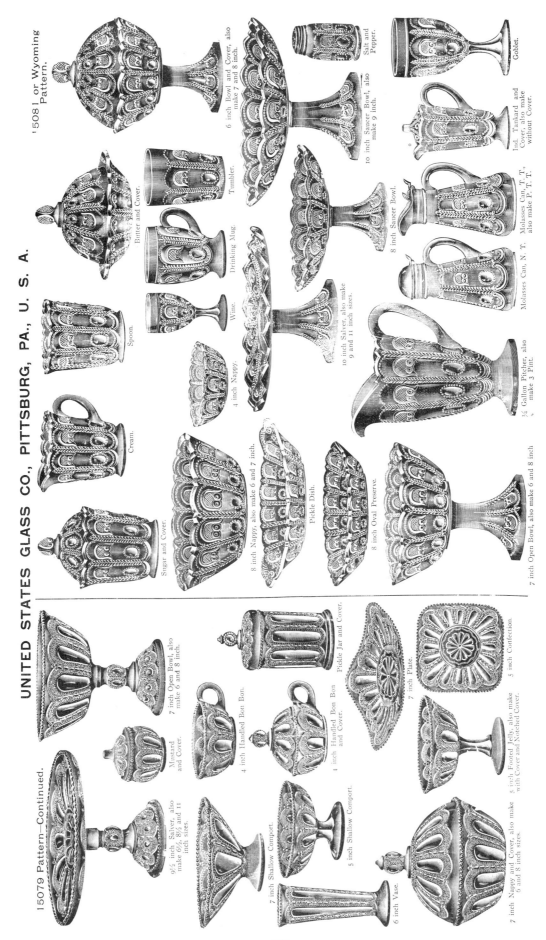

UNITED STATES GLASS CO., PITTSBURG, PA., U. S. A.

'5081 or Wyoming Pattern.

6 inch Bowl and Cover, also make 7 and 8 inch.

Salt and Pepper.

10 inch Saucer Bowl, also make 9 inch.

Goblet.

Butter and Cover.

Tumbler.

Ind. Tankard and Cover, also make without Cover.

Drinking Mug.

8 inch Saucer Bowl.

Molasses Can, T. T., also make P. T. T.

Wine.

Spoon.

Molasses Can, N. T.

Cream.

4 inch Nappy.

10 inch Salver, also make 9 and 11 inch sizes.

½ Gallon Pitcher, also make 3 Pint.

Sugar and Cover.

8 inch Nappy, also make 6 and 7 inch.

Pickle Dish.

8 inch Oval Preserve.

7 inch Open Bowl, also make 6 and 8 inch.

15079 Pattern—Continued.

7 inch Open Bowl, also make 6 and 8 inch.

Pickle Jar and Cover.

7 inch Plate.

5 inch Confection.

Mustard and Cover.

4 inch Handled Bon Bon.

4 inch Handled Bon Bon and Cover.

9½ inch Salver, also make 6½, 8½ and 11 inch sizes.

7 inch Shallow Comport.

5 inch Shallow Comport.

5 inch Footed Jelly, also make with Cover and Notched Cover.

6 inch Vase.

7 inch Nappy and Cover, also make 6 and 8 inch sizes.

151

UNITED STATES GLASS CO., PITTSBURG, PA., U. S. A.

15080 or Utah Pattern.

8 inch Bowl and Cover, also make 6 and 7 inch sizes.

Pickle Dish.

9 inch Salver, also make 7 and 10 inch sizes and 9, 10 and 11 inch Low Salvers.

Oil or Vinegar Bottle.

Tall Celery.

5 inch Footed Jelly and Cover, also make with Notched Cover.

7 inch Bowl, Open, also make 6 and 8 inch sizes and 7½, 9 and 10 inch Saucer Bowls.

Small Butter and Cover, also make with Notched Cover.

2 Bottle Castor.

Molasses Can, T. T., also make P. T. and N. T.

3 Pt. Pitcher.

Butter and Cover.

Goblet.

Spoon Holder.

4 inch Nappy.

Shaker, Salt or Pepper.

6415   3 Pt. Pitcher.

Cream Pitcher.

8 inch Nappy, also make 6 and 7 and same sizes with Covers.

9 inch Oval Dish, also make 7 and 8 inch sizes.

6415 ½ Pt. Tumbler.

Sugar and Cover.

5 inch Footed Jelly, Open.

152

UNITED STATES GLASS CO., PITTSBURG, PA. U. S. A.

15072 or Kansas Pattern.

8 in. High Ft. Bowl and Cover, also make 6 and 7 in. sizes.

5 inch Footed Jelly, Open.

8 in. Low Foot Scolloped Bowl also make 6 and 7 in. sizes.

Molasses Can.

8 inch High Foot Bowl, also make 6 and 7 inch sizes.

Toothpick Holder.

Celery Holder.

For Prices See 1904 List Page No. 87.

9½ in. Fruit Saucer, Footed, also make 7¼ and 8½ in. sizes.

6 inch Footed Sweetmeat and Cover, also make with Notched Cover and without Cover.

Flanged Butter and Cover, also make with Notched Cover.

Pickle Dish.

Salt or Pepper.

5 inch Footed Sweetmeat and Cover, also make with Notched Cover and without Cover.

10 in. High Foot Salver, also make 8 and 9 in. sizes and same sizes with Low Foot.

Butter Dish, also make with Foot, called 7 inch Footed Sweetmeat.

OUR DAILY BREAD

Bread Plate, also make Cake Plate without Lettering.

Illustrations One-third Actual Size.

Wine Glass, also make Goblet.

Spoon holder.

5 inch Footed Jelly and Cover, also make with Notched Cover.

Sugar Bowl.

Cream Pitcher.

8 inch Deep Nappy, also make 4, 6 and 7 inch sizes.

8 inch Preserve Dish.

Handled Mug.

Tumbler.

½ Gallon Pitcher, also make ¾ Gallon.

UNITED STATES GLASS CO., PITTSBURG, PA. U. S. A.

15058 or Missouri Pattern.

7 inch Bowl and Cover, also make 6 and 8 inch sizes.

5 inch Footed Jelly.

9 inch Footed Saucer, also make 8 and 10 inch sizes.

Celery Holder.

Oil or Vinegar Bottle.

5 inch Footed Jelly and Cover, also make with Notched Cover.

Molasses Can, Tin Top.

7 inch Bowl, also make 6 and 8 inch sizes.

6 inch Footed Jelly. Flared.

Olive Dish.

Goblet.

10 inch Salver, also make 9 and 11 inch sizes.

Butter Dish.

Wine.

Pickle Dish.

Cordial.

Spoon Holder.

Shaker, Salt or Pepper.

½ Gal. Pitcher, also make ¼ Gal. Illustration ¼ actual size.

Cream Pitcher.

Handled Mug.

Tumbler.

8 inch Nappy, also make 4, 6 and 7 inch sizes.

Sugar Bowl.

7 inch Nappy and Cover, also make 6 and 8 inch sizes.

Oval Dish.

Bread Plate.

154

UNITED STATES GLASS CO. PITTSBURG, PA., U. S. A.

15064 or Tennessee Pattern.

7 inch Footed Bowl and Cover, also make 6 and 8 inch sizes.

Handled Mug.

9 inch Footed Bowl also make 8 and 10 inch sizes.

5 inch Footed Jelly and Cover.

5 inch Footed Jelly.

Round Bread Plate.

6 in. Footed Bowl, also make 7 and 8 in. sizes.

8½ inch Salver, also make 9½ and 10½ inch sizes.

Celery Holder.

Toothpick Holder.

Shaker, Salt or Pepper.

½ Gal. Pitcher, also make ¼ Gal. Illustration ¼ actual size.

Butter Dish.

Pickle Dish.

Oil or Vinegar Bottle.

Tumbler.

Spoon Holder.

4 inch Nappy.

Molasses Can.

Goblet.

Wine Glass.

Cream Pitcher.

Sugar Bowl.

8 inch Nappy, also make 6 and 7 inch sizes.

8 inch Preserve Dish.

8 inch Nappy and Cover, also make 6 and 7 inch sizes.

155

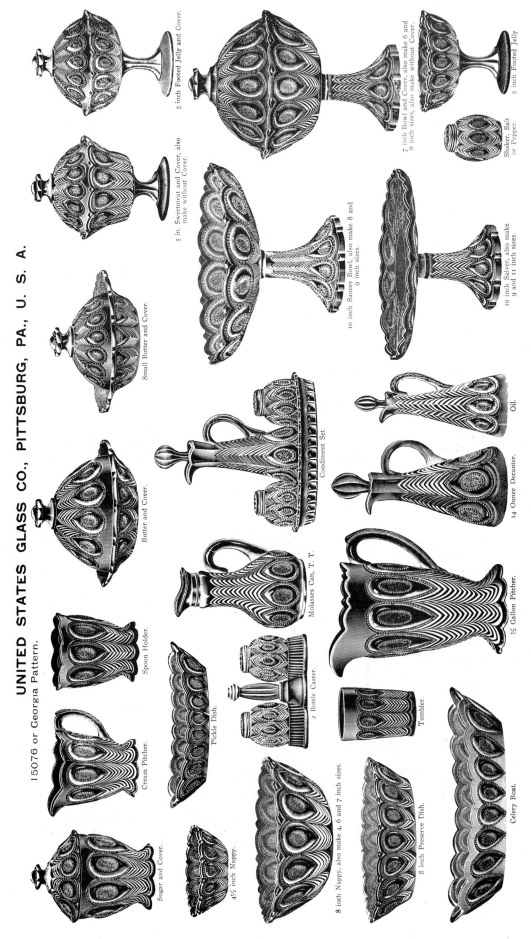

UNITED STATES GLASS CO., PITTSBURG, PA., U. S. A.

15076 or Georgia Pattern.

5 inch Footed Jelly and Cover.

5 in. Sweetmeat and Cover, also make without Cover.

7 inch Bowl and Cover, also make 6 and 8 inch sizes, also make without Cover.

5 inch Footed Jelly.

Shaker, Salt or Pepper.

Small Butter and Cover.

10 inch Saucer Bowl, also make 8 and 9 inch sizes.

10 inch Salver, also make 9 and 11 inch sizes.

Butter and Cover.

Condiment Set.

Oil.

14 Ounce Decanter.

Spoon Holder.

Molasses Can, T. T.

½ Gallon Pitcher.

Cream Pitcher.

Pickle Dish.

2 Bottle Caster.

Tumbler.

Sugar and Cover.

4½ inch Nappy.

8 inch Nappy, also make 4, 6 and 7 inch sizes.

8 inch Preserve Dish.

Celery Boat.

156